POETICS OF HISTORY

FORDHAM UNIVERSITY PRESS   NEW YORK 2019

POETICS OF HISTORY

*Rousseau and the Theater
of Originary Mimesis*

PHILIPPE LACOUE-LABARTHE

Translated by Jeff Fort

This book was originally published in French as Philippe
Lacoue-Labarthe, *Poétique de l'histoire*, Copyright © Éditions
Galilée, 2002.

Cet ouvrage a bénéficié du soutien des Programmes d'aide à la
publication de l'Institut Français.

This work, published as part of a program of aid for publication, received support from the Institut Français.

Ouvrage publié avec le concours du Ministère français chargé
de la Culture–Centre National du Livre.

This work has been published with the assistance of the French
Ministry of Culture–National Center for the Book.

Library of Congress Cataloging-in-Publication Data available
online at https://catalog.loc.gov.

Printed in the United States of America

21   20   19   5   4   3   2   1

First edition

to Christine and François,
Mathilde and Pascal

and to the memory of Philippe Clévenot,
actor

CONTENTS

Frequens imitatio transit in mores

QUINTILIAN

PART ONE

The Scene of Origin

1

During the winter semester of 1934–1935, in circumstances of which we are well aware, Heidegger for the first time included Hölderlin in his teaching program. For his commentary he chose—very deliberately, one imagines—two of the great completed hymns: *Germania* and *The Rhine*. Bound up in the anxious archipolitical question, "Who are we?" (implicitly: we Germans), the message of this course was unequivocal: Hölderlin alone holds the secret of Germanness or of the Germanic (to translate *das Deutsche*); only by listening to his Poem would it be possible to rectify the National Socialist deviation and to found in truth the Revolution that is in the process of being aborted. For this revolution is based on a philosophical proposition that is equally clear, through which, with respect to History, the properly transcendental status of Poetry (*Dichtung*) is established: Poetry, that is, art in its essence, inextricably composed of language and myth (*Sprache und Sage*), is the condition of possibility, or the origin, of History as such—or, if you prefer, of the unveiling of Being in terms of existence. A few months later, in the lectures on "The Origin of the Work of Art," this proposition will receive its canonical form: the work of art is the thesis of truth (of *alētheia*). From the courses of 1934–1935, I cite, for example, only these few statements:

> The Historial Dasein of the peoples—its rise, its pinnacle, and its decline—springs from poetry, and from this a proper knowing in the sense of philosophy, and from both the effecting of the Dasein of a people as a people through the state: politics. This originary, historical time of the peoples is therefore the time of the poets, thinkers, and creators of the state—that is, of those who properly ground and found the historial Dasein of a people.

Or again:

> Poetizing founds Beyng. Poetizing is the primordial language of a people. Within such language, there occurs a being-exposed to beings which thereby open themselves up. As the accomplishment of such exposure, the human being is historial. The human being "has" a history only because and to the extent that he is historial. Language is the ground of the possibility of history, but language is not something like an invention that is first made within the course of the history of cultural creations.[1]

It is not too difficult to perceive that, under the preoccupation with History or historicity (or historiality), what is at work here is a complete reelaboration of the Greek problem of the relation between *phusis* and *tekhnē*: "Nature and Art," as Hölderlin still says, Saturn and Jupiter, or, following a lexicon that he shares with Schelling, "aorgic" and "organic"; Heidegger, for his part, will call them Earth and World. This is all the more evident when, right after the passage I just quoted, Heidegger continues with an entire development dedicated, as the editors' subtitle indicates, to "The Absence of Language in the Animal and in 'Nature'"—a theme, furthermore, that recurs regularly in his thought and that is linked, as we know, to the determination of man as mortal, that is, as alone capable of death:

> The originary origin of language as the essential ground of human Dasein, however, remains a mystery. Especially when we ponder the fact that even where there is "life" (plant, animal), language does not also occur without further ado, even if it seems as though it were merely a matter of eliminating some persistent inhibition in order for the animal to speak. And yet! The leap from living animal to the human being who tells is just as great as, or still greater than, that from the lifeless stone to the living. (HH 75/68)

A little further on he adds, leaving no doubt about the fundamental aim of his argument,

Yet this apparent nearness and at the same time essential distance of the animal to the human first becomes a genuine question when we give thought to the real absence of language that we find in nature as a whole, where, on the other hand, nothing can "speak" more insistently to us than the prevailing of nature in its greater and in its smallest aspects.

That is to say, we will not succeed simply by placing nature with its absence of language and human beings who speak alongside one another as different kinds of things. We shall first approach our questioning here if we ponder fundamentally how poetizing as the fundamental event of the historial Dasein of human beings relates—if we may put things this way at all—to *nature*, prior to all natural science. The whole of natural science—indispensable though it is within certain present-day limits . . . for all its exactness leaves us fundamentally in the lurch here regarding what is essential, because it de-'natures' nature. (HH 75–76/68–69)

I will defer all commentary for the moment. What I would like to indicate to begin with, however, is this: it is on the basis of such a claim—a claim that is so to speak absolutely paradoxical—of the originating or transcendental nature of *tekhnē* (language and poetry, or language as poetry) that Heidegger undertakes a reading of the poem "The Rhine" and, in this poem, of its tenth strophe. This strophe is well known for being one of the most remarkable places where Hölderlin invokes the name of

Rousseau (itself associated, in a way that is far from indifferent, with that of Dionysos, which remains unspoken there).

I read it here, for the sake of convenience, in its most "readable" translation:

Of demigods now I think
And I must know these dear ones,
Because often their lives
So move my longing breast.
Yet he whose soul, like yours,
Rousseau, became invincible,
The strongly enduring,
And in its sense assured
And sweet in its gift of hearing,
Of talking so that out of holy fullness he
Like the wine god, foolishly divinely
And lawlessly bestows it, the language of the
    purest,
Understandable for the good, yet rightly strikes
With blindness the irreverent,
The profaning slaves, how shall I name the stranger?[2]

And this is Heidegger's commentary:

What this strophe tells of is only a question, and remains only a question: namely, that concerning the stranger. Who is this stranger, this one who remains strange? In this strophe we find the name "Rousseau." We know that his name was inserted only later, in place of the name of Hölderlin's friend, Heinse [Wilhelm Heinse, the author of *Ardinghello* and the dedicatee of the elegy "Bread and Wine"]. In strophe XI, line 163, the words "by the Bielersee" are likewise a later addition that, in reference to the naming of Rousseau, mentions his place of residence. An original interpretation of the strophe must therefore be kept clear of reference to Rousseau; conversely, it is only in terms of the meaning of the strophe that we can come to understand why the poet can also name Rousseau here. (HH 277–278/251 [Lacoue-Labarthe's interpolation])[3]

Duly noted, one might say; in fact, we will learn no more about it. Admittedly, in the context of the 1930s, this exclusion is frequent. It occurs quite regularly, in any case, in Heidegger's courses. The fact is that Rousseau is the (reviled) representative of "liberal" thought (Rousseau, in other words, as a stand-in for Cassirer, if I may be allowed a short-cut). Doubtless, too, Heidegger takes care to moderate the brutality of his gesture. Having established that "the being that is here named in questioning" is linked with "Nature," he specifies:

The essence of such a primordial beyng uninterrupted in its naturalness, suggests the thought of Rousseau and his doctrine, although here we must still ponder the fact that that particular era—roughly that of Kant and German Idealism—regarded Rousseau quite differently from how we do today. Yet none of this is of primary importance here. (HH 278/252)[4]

Nevertheless, the exclusion is without appeal—and we clearly see, furthermore, that the regret (only roughly suggested, in terms of Rousseau and his "doctrine") in reality only makes things worse. Indeed, the exclusion is clearly reiterated; and if we pay just a little attention to the justifications provided it becomes evident that this exclusion is not only political, as is often the case elsewhere (out of hatred for the French Revolution, democracy, rule of law, etc.), but properly philosophical: even the interpretation of Kant and of German Idealism cannot save Rousseau from his doctrinal, if not doctrinaire, weakness, namely, the metaphysical inadequacy of his thought on the aforementioned "Nature." The concept of "Nature," which Hölderlin indeed largely inherited from Rousseau, is in reality—Heidegger often returns to this point—what nearly led him astray and blocked his path to a "more original" notion of *phusis*, or Earth. The "rescue" of Hölderlin (his *Rettung*, to use Benjamin's term) comes at the price of this emphatic distancing from Rousseau. And we grasp fairly easily what is at stake in this maneuver: it is the same as what is at stake in *all* of Heidegger's thought, insofar as this thought is fundamentally concerned with the originary nature of *tekhnē*. Insofar, then, as this thought cannot find support in a derivative, weak, overly elementary and naive determination of *phusis*—of "Nature," in its Latin (and French) concept, but also, probably, its Kantian-Schillerian one.

The thesis that I propose to defend, then, is that here, with regard to Rousseau, there is a blindness. The bias, the ill will, or the lack of credit granted by Heidegger (when he devotes such elaborate efforts, precisely, to tearing Kant and Hölderlin, or even Schiller, away from the "spirit of the Enlightenment"—though all three drew heavily on Rousseau—or from their misinterpretation in the 19th century, by Schopenhauer in particular[5]), in short, the refusal to read (a "political" refusal): these are not the only aspects in question. Heidegger, in reality, does not *perceive* Rousseau. And if he does not perceive him, it is because his (Heidegger's) historiography forbids him to do so. Twice over.

The first time, it is because this historiography depends deeply on the Hegelian historiography that locates the destinal turning-point of the modern in the Cartesian, or Galilean-Cartesian moment (the installation of representative certainty, the identification of being with the subject, as *ego cogito*, the objective mathematization of physics, which has become the science of nature, the programming of technoscience, etc.). Rousseau's belonging to this era of thought is patent, as evidenced by his fidelity to Malebranche, his avowal of ethico-theological faith, or his political theory of the general will. The entire question is to know whether Rousseau belongs only to this era, and if rather more secret links tie him to an antiquity not limited to that of Plutarch or of Saint Augustine;[6] or if the "withdrawal" of which he makes himself the example without example does not decisively draw him out of his era or does not constitute the very heart of his thought itself as an era or "epoch."

A second time, because in this Hegelian-inspired historiography, the only destinal event that Heidegger recognizes within the Modern Age is the (German) invention of history and of the thought of historicity, which is to say of the historial character of being and of truth. He evokes Winckelmann several times (whose *Gedanken*[7] are exactly contemporaneous with Rousseau's second *Discourse* [the *Discourse on Inequality*, 1754]), and Herder;[8] he is obviously invoking German idealism in its entirety, up to Burckhardt and Nietzsche. It is to Herder, in any case, that another seminar is dedicated in 1934–1936, and from whom Heidegger draws the guiding idea on the origin of languages and the essence of language as the originary poetry of peoples. That Rousseau might be at the source of such a thinking of history (or, and it amounts to the same thing, of origin), that he could have been recognized as such by all of German philosophy—this does not interest him for a second. Rousseau therefore has no role to play in the invention of the thinking of history and, in any case, he is probably not a "thinker."

This blindness—and this is my thesis—would then in reality be Heidegger's blind spot.

Two hypotheses, as is fitting, must support this thesis.

The first, which has guided my work for a long time, consists in the suspicion that it is a reinterpretation of *mimēsis*, unavowed or denied, that underpins the Heideggerian notion of *tekhnē*, notwithstanding the contempt displayed on occasion regarding this concept—judged, as we know, to be belated or derivative, subordinated to the understanding of truth as *homoiōsis*, strained by its Latin translation into *imitatio*, etc. The clearest indicator of this dissimulation lies in the simple fact that, at bottom, it is to Aristotle—always placed, admittedly, under the authority of the canonical statement of Heraclitus: *phusis kruptesthai philei*, "nature loves to hide"—that Heidegger turns in order to penetrate the secret of the originally Greek comprehension of *phusis* and its relationship to *tekhnē* (I am thinking of the great and meticulous reading, carried out in the period 1930–1940, of the *Physics* B, 1, which will remain determinative for all the texts that followed),[9] never, to my knowledge, does he turn to the *Poetics*, nor even to the two major propositions concerning *tekhnē* in the *Physics* (in B, 2 and B, 8), which remained guiding principles for the entire Western conception of art and technics.

I recall these propositions here because, no less than *phusis kruptesthai philei*, they govern, in very precise fashion, knowingly or not, Rousseau's thought. Especially the second (199a), which is ordinarily said to explicate the first: *hē tekhnē mimeitai tēn phusin* (194a), and which states: *tekhnē*

> *ta men epitelei ha hē phusis adunatei apergasasthai, ta de mimeitai.*

Which we might translate (I refer to the translation by Jean Beaufret, who cites this proposition precisely in interpreting the Hölderlinian thought of the relation between "art" and "nature"[10]): "On the one hand, art brings to term [we might also say: finishes (L-L)] what nature is unable to operate [to work: *oeuvrer*], on the other hand, it imitates." And we see clearly, now, that the entire difficulty comes from the use of this verb: *apergasasthai* (to work) regarding *phusis*. And, not surprisingly, the word *ergon* and the concept of *energeia* have an important place in the Heideggerian commentary of the *Physics*.[11] But everything proceeds—and here, therefore, is the suspicion—as if he were passing too quickly over this difficulty, as if he were rushing to make a sharp distinction, and to decide that *ergon*, in essence, does not belong to doing or making (*machen*) but to producing and installing (*herstellen*), ontologically determined as "bringing into presence" or "into presentation."

There is much to say about this precipitousness; I will return to it later. For the moment, in a provisional and simply indicative way, I will confine myself to mentioning that this is very probably what dictates to Heidegger his riskiest statements about poetry or the essence of the work of art (which, as we know from the lectures of 1935 and 1936 on "The Origin of the Work of Art," must be thought of not as *Darstellung*, which is to say *mimēsis* or (re)presentation, but as putting to work and thesis— *Gestell*—of the truth, of *alētheia*, of *phusis* insofar as it likes to "crypt" itself).[12] I will pick up only one of them,

which leaves us in proximity to Hölderlin—and, consequently, to Rousseau. It is found, again, in the commentary on "The Rhine." Heidegger seeks to apprehend the
content of the verb *ahnen*, "to have a presentiment" or
"to intimate," which Hölderlin uses when he speaks of
Nature "intimating" or when he says that poets "intimate"; he asks therefore about this tonality or fundamental disposition, about this *Stimmung* which he describes
as "that arousing-restrained attunement in which the
mystery opens itself as such, spreading out in its entire
expanses and yet folding itself together into one."
He then says:

> Because the poets are not directed toward nature as
> an object, for instance; because, rather, "nature" as
> beyng founds itself in saying, the saying of the poets
> as the self-saying of nature is of the same essence
> as the latter. (HH 257/233)

The second hypothesis therefore concerns Rousseau;
this is the hypothesis that, to begin with, I will work to
justify. The political or archipolitical reasons that bring
Heidegger to scorn the "liberal" thought that claims
Rousseau as something of a founding hero, are beyond
doubtful (I have written elsewhere about the archifas-
cism of Heidegger[13]). It remains the case that these reasons accentuate, at least in part, that which in the classic
interpretation of Rousseau (and it makes little difference
whether this interpretation is rationalist or not), remains
notoriously inadequate: as long as, indeed, we conceive

of Rousseau in terms of what he himself, from the beginning, or very nearly, calls his "*sistême*"; as long as we see this system culminate, beyond the pedagogical project or the ethico-metaphysical profession of faith, in the political theory of the *Social Contract* (or see it alter itself, which amounts to the same thing, while also producing a whole new possibility for literature, the autobiographical or fictional project); as long, in fact, as we do not question with sufficient rigor that which is unfathomably problematic in the Rousseauian concept of "nature" (and, correlatively, in that of "existence"), we risk misrecognizing, to various degrees, that which makes the absolute originality of Rousseau and which is, precisely, his thought of the *origin*.

Assuredly, as Heidegger concedes, German Idealism did read Rousseau more deeply than did, in the same period, French revolutionary thought or, later on, "liberal" thought. But to point out, for example, that "Kantian morals" presuppose Rousseau or, more decisively, that Kant's philosophy of history (and then that of Schiller, with everything that follows)[14] is derived from the (pre) dialectical logic that commands the relationship established by Rousseau between Nature and Culture, does not go deeply enough. In reality, what is at stake in the *thought of the origin* is the very thing that Heidegger, *at one and the same time*, denies and allows to be seen, and *first of all* in his teachings on Hölderlin: namely, that the thought of the origin is at the origin of *both* the thought of the transcendental (in the Kantian sense) *and* the thought of negativity (in the dialectical-speculative sense). Or, more rigorously formulated, that it is at the origin of the thought of the transcendental *as* the thought of negativity. And there, indeed, is the basis, in effect, of the *Auseinandersetzung*, of the controversy or the explication, engaged by Heidegger with the "great German philosophy," as he says, and, behind it, with all of Western metaphysics.

2

To take the measure of stakes such as these, we must attempt to grasp, in its origin, the thought of the origin. In the very blow that is its sendoff its *coup d'envoi*.

I will wager that this blow is struck, or delivered, in the very first pages of the *Discourse on the Origin and Foundations of Inequality Among Men*. Definitively, but imperceptibly, so to speak, or in a barely audible fashion. And that, beyond this—within this same text, as in subsequent elaborations (in the *Essay on the Origin of Languages* as well as in the *Social Contract*), in the problematic of the origin, as Rousseau indeed is able to thematize it, not to say systematize it, and therefore as we will understand it according to the evidence—this blow will no longer resound except in a very deadened way, beneath the clamor of a "doctrine," as Heidegger says.

What exactly happens, then, at the beginning of the second *Discourse*? (For the sake of my specific purposes, I condense—abusively, no doubt—analyses that would require more ample and detailed treatment and justifications.[1])

First of all, we must consider, and in all seriousness, the fact that Rousseau offers his response to the question posed by the Academy of Dijon as a *properly philosophical* response. He does this twice: already, in the first paragraph of the Preface, where the explicit reference to Buffon (which is the subject of a note), and the implicit one to Malebranche,[2] should not mask the essential, namely the reminder of the inaugural Delphic-Socratic precept of philosophy as such and the allusion to the statue of Glaucus in Book X of Plato's *Republic* (that is, to the very image of *disfiguration*):

> The most useful and the least advanced of all human knowledge seems to me to be that of man; and I dare say that the inscription on the Temple at Delphi alone, contained a more important and more difficult Precept than all the big Books of the Moralists. I therefore consider the subject of this Discourse to be one of the most interesting questions that Philosophy might raise and, unfortunately for us, one of the thorniest that Philosophers might have to resolve. For how can the source of inequality among men be known, without first knowing men themselves? And how will man ever succeed in seeing himself as nature formed him, through all the changes which the

succession of times and things must have wrought in his original constitution, and to disentangle what he owes to his own stock from what circumstances and his progress have added to or changed in his primitive state? Like the statue of Glaucus which time, sea, and storms had so disfigured that it less resembled a God than a ferocious Beast, the human soul, altered in the lap of society by a thousand forever recurring causes, by the acquisition of a mass of knowledge and errors, by the changes that have taken place in the constitution of Bodies, and by the continual impact of the passions, has, so to speak, changed in appearance to the point of being almost unrecognizable. (DI, 129)

When Rousseau says, after having dispatched with a single stroke "all the fat Books of the Moralists," that he considers "the subject of this *Discourse* to be one of the most interesting questions that Philosophy might raise," it is consequently clear that he is not thinking of the "*Philosophes*" (his contemporaries) but of the entirety of philosophy since its acknowledged beginning. Next, in the preliminary or the exordium, where he reports the strictly aporetic nature, up to that point, of the question of the origin ("The Philosophers who have examined the foundations of society have all felt the necessity of going back as far as the state of Nature, but none of them has reached it" [DI, 139]), and where he announces (in a way that Kant will remember) his intention—indeed a critical intention—to put an end to the infinite conflict of hypotheses or unfounded extrapolations, it is no less clear that there is no restriction here to the field of "political philosophy," but that Rousseau takes a frontal approach to one of the founding oxymorons of philosophy, the *zōon politikon phusei*, which moreover he will associate, in all rigor, with the *zōon logon ekhōn* (I will return to this question). We must not misunderstand the declaration of intention, which, in the exordium, precedes the final address to "Man": it is the affirmation of the *philosophical* itself.

> Since my subject concerns man in general, I shall try to speak in a language suited to all nations, or rather, forgetting times and Places in order to think only about the Men to whom I speak, I shall suppose myself in the Lyceum of Athens, repeating the Lessons of my Masters, with such men as Plato and Xenocrates for Judges, and Mankind for an Audience. (DI, 140)

All this amounts to saying (first conclusion) that the question of the origin—"one of the thorniest that Philosophers might have to resolve," meaning, the most difficult—is, quite simply, poorly formulated. This is the true starting point for Rousseau. And this, then, is the task he assigns himself in his first pages: to reelaborate entirely this question *as* a question; to pose, with new efforts, and on other bases, *the question of this question*. This preliminary gesture, inscribed, no doubt, like all those of the period, in the Cartesian tradition of the return to the foundation, of the search for a primary certainty (we know that this will always haunt Rousseau), is *also*, in a mode as yet unknown, a veritable "step back" *into* the question—which, however, his contemporaries will misinterpret in caricatural and crude fashion, without seeing that in reality it is a chasm opening (and never ceasing to open) beneath Rousseau's feet. But Rousseau, for his part, is perfectly conscious, as he always will be ("I am forming an enterprise which has had no example") that he is innovating. The obligatory modesty of the statement does not at any moment hide this complete clearsightedness:

> Let my Readers therefore not imagine that I dare flatter myself with having seen what seems to me so difficult to see. I have initiated some arguments; I have hazarded some conjectures, less in the hope of resolving the question than with the intention of elucidating it and reducing it to its true state. (DI, 130)

What, consequently, does *origin* mean?

In order to gain access to a rigorous answer, it is necessary to recognize a certain terminological instability (source, beginning(s), cause, principle, foundation(s), nature, state of nature, primitive state, earliest times, etc.); just as it will very obviously be necessary to recognize, at the proper moment, to what extent this instability indeed betrays the impossibility for Rousseau to remain within the register he imposed on himself at the start, and which forces him to yield to a fiction of origins (for want of an empirical deduction of beginnings). This is relatively secondary, except, probably, for the future of literature—I mean, for *literature*, which Rousseau perhaps inaugurates *as such*.

Origin, in a word that Rousseau does not use, designates purely and simply *essence*.

In taking on the oxymoron of the *zōon politikon phusei*, in setting himself the task of breaking it, Rousseau asks himself the question of knowing what man is *phusei*, man "in his nature," as he says indeed, or in his "original constitution." We cannot forget that the general epigraph of the *Discourse* is drawn from Aristotle's *Politics*, and that it says—I quote the translation offered by Starobinski, "What is natural must be sought not in beings that are depraved, but in those who comport themselves in conformity with nature."[3] The gesture therefore appears to be quite classic—and so it is indeed, in that, once again, it takes the form of a search for a foundation or, under the problematic horizon that is necessarily Rousseau's (that of political philosophy or of the philosophy of law), with the search for an anteriority, for a "state" that is presocial, prepolitical or precivil, preconventional, prehistorical, etc., which will inevitably give rise to the historico-genetic inquiry, meaning, to a relatively weak interpretation of the inaugural oxymoron, as attested, upon an initial reading at least, by the famous maxim: "Man is sociable by nature, or at least made to become so."[4] And besides, as the doxography has clearly shown, Rousseau repeats, sometimes almost to the word, statements or arguments that he borrows from his vast readings, from Cicero to Hobbes and Montesquieu, from Herodotus and Pliny to Pufendorf or Grotius.

Now if I have translated "origin" as "essence," in the Heideggerian sense of the term, it is not only in thinking of the strange resonance of the word "source" in Hölderlin's and Heidegger's *Ur-sprung*; it is in order to take account of the radicalization that Rousseau effects in this reopening of the question of the origin *as a question*.

This radicalization can be approached in three ways:

1. According to the logic of essence itself, which is to say, this logic that commands that the essence of a thing is *nothing* of that thing.

That man in his actuality should be able to define himself—in the order of observation or of facticity—as a social, political, historical (etc.) being is precisely what forbids us from thinking him such in his essence or nature, in the Aristotelian sense. It is this logic that gives the principle of the truly *critical* intention that governs the Preface and the exordium, directed as they are by the demand to "disentangle what is original from what is artificial in man's present nature" (DI, 130): hence the description of the *Kampfplatz* of theories of natural justice, or of their attempts at a "metaphysical" foundation (DI, 131); hence the declaration of the inanity of the concept of "Natural Law" (DI, 132); hence the idea of a subtraction without remainder of every acquired feature, or even a deconstruction of the "Edifice" of "human establishments" (DI, 134) or, and this amounts to the same thing, a *cleansing* and *restoration* of the statue of Glaucus; hence, too, the denunciation of the projections, reckonings, question-beggings extrapolations, etc. Beneath the search for a *pure* nature, or a sort of "pure text" of nature—in fact drawn directly from the protestant tradition of "textual critique"—there is this pure paradox: the essence (the origin) is *absolutely* prior, logically and not only chronologically, to all the determinations of man as a being of culture, including those that appear most "natural": family, morality, language or reason (understanding). The essence of culture (of *tekhnē*) is nothing cultural, nothing technical. But an abyss—a hiatus—*also* separates Nature from Culture. It is this that will lead, unfailingly, to the denaturing of human nature that we have often emphasized, if only because it opens the possibility of an ontologization of History. The *de-natured* being of man is his being-historical. In principle and immediately. (It would remain to be seen why, regarding man, nature is originally *denatured* or *denaturing*: what is the originary *defect* or *lack* [*défaut*] of nature? Rousseau does not seem to provide an answer; nor does he even pose the question in clear terms. We will try to come back to it: it is a question with nothing to support it.)

2. According to the logic of the *arkhē*, or the archeological.

By virtue of its very ab-soluteness, the origin is deemed inaccessible—in practice if not (totally) in principle—

or even purely hypothetical. Where Pufendorf, for example, being relatively prudent, limited himself to saying of the state of nature that it "never . . . existed in any present except in part and with some moderation," Rousseau, for his part, speaks of "a state which no longer exists, which perhaps never did exist, which probably never will exist" (DI, 130); and he immediately adds, "and about which it is nevertheless necessary to have exact Notions in order accurately to judge of our present state." As he will write later to M. de Beaumont: "this [originary] man does not exist . . . granted. But he can exist by supposition."[5] It is in obeying this logic that Rousseau states that he has "ventured some conjectures" or "hypothetical and conditional reasonings" (DI, 139). It is nevertheless necessary to grasp the fact that no empirical or even experimental route, in the taste of the era—in the Marivaux of *The Dispute*, for example (DI, 53–54)—is viable here (hence the refusal of "all the facts" [DI, 139]) and that the supposition represents a veritable *leap* into the origin, with no other support—if it is a support—than a "self," that is, the nature in "me": sentiment or interior evidence, attestation of the heart, "lived" evidence. The gesture—exactly like its belated corollary in the "Second Walk" of the *Reveries*: the pure grasping of existence—is without precedent, from the very fact that no certainty, as remains after all in Cartesian doubt, and no assurance from reason directs or halts it. The intuition of the origin, of "nature," is properly vertiginous.

3. According to a transcendental logic.

In truth, no logic of this kind precedes Rousseau's gesture; rather it is indeed this gesture that produces this logic—and which, historically, will have produced it. What Rousseau seeks in the origin ("nature") is the possibility of what bars it, or has barred it. That this possibility should therefore also be the possibility of its other, or of its others (culture, institution, reason, history; in short, everything that belongs to the realm of *tekhnē*), this is not in doubt. But what is excluded is that this possibility might be its *cause*. In other words, in its very ab-soluteness the origin is not without a connection to that of which it is the origin, otherwise it would not be the origin and its absoluteness would not be an absoluteness (this is the argument of Hegel against Kant). But the origin does not relate to that of which it is the origin as to its effect or its consequence. From itself to that of which it is the origin, there is rupture, hiatus. The origin is nothing of that of which it is the origin. This amounts quite simply to saying that the origin is thought neither as cause nor even, in reality, as foundation (at least in the most radical register that Rousseau enters), rather the origin is thought as *condition*—de jure, and not de facto. This is why it is—and is only—the *negative* of that of which it is the origin. The very "formula" of the transcendental, "condition of possibility," will express it perfectly. The *condition*, which is strictly *nothing*, pure negativity ("pure form," as Kant will say, finding no other term), opens *possibility* itself (position, positing, or positivity).[6] What Rousseau discovers or invents is the transcendental as negativity itself, or, if you prefer: *transcendental negativity*. One could also say, as Hölderlin does, "mediacy," which is the (transcendental) "Law" of the impossibility of the immediate. Hegel, in any case, in his faithful infidelity to Kant, will remember this; but the affair will still resonate even in Heidegger's finite transcendence.

In its broadest generality, the law that Rousseau establishes states that, in an absolute paradox, *phusis* is the condition of possibility of *tekhnē*. This law—the transcendental law itself—produces, in turn, a fundamental thesis: man, in that he is originarily *tekhnitēs*, is not an animal, that is, a living being endowed in addition with this or that quality. The nature of man is not to have a nature. Or, if you like: Man is not a being of nature, but a being originarily lacking or in default of nature. He is, according to an oxymoron that is completely different from the one passed down by the tradition, a denatured animal. Which is to say—but this is not the place to insist on the point (I will try to say more about this elsewhere)—a nonliving living being. A "mortal," says Heidegger. Which is to say an "immortal," as Blanchot will add.[7]

It is true that Rousseau recoils before his own discovery, that is, before this abyss. His formulations, in any case, betray not a prudence, as is always claimed, but a perplexity. It is in sum too difficult to think man without animal. Or even, in the end, an originary denaturation of nature, which is perhaps the abyss of all of meta-*physics*, in whatever sense we understand the word. It is indeed, however, at the edge of this thought that he stands. After having said, for example, at the very beginning of Part I:

> By stripping the Being, so constituted, of all the super-natural gifts he may have received, and of all the ar-tificial faculties he could only have acquired by prolonged progress; by considering him, in a word, such as he must have issued from the hands of Nature, I see an animal less strong than some, less agile than others, but, all things considered, the most advanta-geously organized of all ... (DI, 141)

Rousseau specifies, a few pages later:

> Savage Man, left by Nature to bare instinct alone, or rather, compensated for any lack of instinct by facul-ties capable of making up for it [*suppléer*] at first, and of afterwards raising him far above nature, will then begin with purely animal functions ... (DI, 149)

Twice over, as we see, Rousseau defines man negatively: a less strong and agile animal (but the comparative tem-pers the negativity), an animal lacking or in default (*en défaut*) of instinct, that is, in default of animality. But twice over, the statement vacillates: it immediately sup-poses man to possess a more advantageous "organ-ization" (we are in the lexicon, which Aristotle exploited, of *ergon* and of *organon*), or an originary faculty of "making up for" or "supplementing [*suppléer*]." And we are indeed entering, in the register of the "quasi-transcendental," into the logic of the supplement that Jacques Derrida so rigorously analyzed, and which we see, without the slightest difficulty, wholly inscribed in the mimetology derived from Aristotle. *Tekhnē* is thought here as an *excess* [*un surcroît*] of *phusis*.

This is moreover what constrains Rousseau—between a transcendental deduction (a dreaded task) and an empirical deduction (which he refuses)—to choose the middle path of the fiction of origins, that is, of a beginning and a transition, even if this moment must, as rigor demands, remain unassignable or referred, miraculously, to some natural accident (when not quite simply to divine will[8]). We would need to study from this angle, and with great precision, how the transcendental present is constantly subordinated to the modalization of the narrative past; or how—and this amounts to the same thing—the hiatus between Nature and Culture is reduced to being no more than "a great divide" (DI, 151; translation modified).

But this is again what produces the weak version of the transcendental, which will remain—inevitably—the major theorem of the "doctrine": man is absolutely distinguished from animal by these two original qualities or virtualities that compose something like the *vis dormitiva* of his humanity, freedom and perfectibility—though the affirmation of "freedom" is explicitly directed against the determination of man as *rational animal*:

"It is then not so much the understanding that constitutes the specific difference between man and the other animals, as it is his property of being a free agent" (DI, 148). There is no doubt that it is indeed from here, essentially, that the transcendental reflection on history, in any case that of Kant, will be organized. But there is likewise no doubt that, with respect to the question of the origin, this point is not the most decisive. Freedom and perfectibility are notions on which Rousseau bases himself when he speaks, already, the language of results and sets out on the path that leads to the "system." It is not by chance that these notions underlie the construction of *The Social Contract*. Previously, however, in the first intuition, Rousseau uses a completely different, and more radical, language. And it is obviously this language that interests me, because it is there that we see emerge, by virtue of its initial [*primitive*] audacity, the transcendental problematic, and it is there that this problematic arrives as one of originary *tekhnē*—and not of morality or of originary civility. I will thus allow myself, for this reason, to speak of *onto-technology*.

3

The animality of man is not really what holds Rousseau's attention. In the order of narration, or of conjecture, the affair is quickly dispatched. There is little to say about the supposed "State of Nature," except that in the immobility of a null time, the man-animal, as a simply living being (the *zōon*), as a being of need, is immediately satisfied: "I see him sating his hunger beneath an oak, slaking his thirst at the first Stream, finding his bed at the foot of the same tree that supplied his meal, and with that his needs are satisfied" (DI 141–142). We need not give much importance here to the detailed discussion that Rousseau engages with Malebranche, Buffon, Condillac, La Mettrie—among others—concerning the animal-machine, sensation and the passions, the birth of ideas, and so on. What is important, however, is that if the state of nature is thus the state of immediate satisfaction, the man-animal is nonetheless, compared to the

"Beasts," absolutely inferior. It is even precisely because he is inferior (he is, in short, a sub-animal) that he is able to satisfy his properly animal or vital needs. The one reserve being that it is in the mode not of elementary or *physical* life, but of what we must indeed call a sur-vival (*sur-vie*), that is, *meta*-physical life, or, what amounts to the same, *technical* life.[1]

When he introduces the idea of an originary lack in man, of an essential defect (*défaut*) of nature—and what is at issue is indeed a defect or lack of all *proper instinct*—Rousseau immediately carries out two analyses.

The first, which in reality comes second, has to do with the "body of the Savage Man," that is, of the animal whose very nudity binds it to force and robustness, to the *energy* that is the first condition of survival. Rousseau—very attentive, from the start, to the historicity of the body, to the "changes that have taken place in the constitution of Bodies" (129)—speaks then of the body of the savage man as the "only tool which [he] knows" (142), a machine (in the Greek sense) or industry (in the Latin sense) predating any machine or industry: primitive paradoxical *tekhnē*, naturally a-natural, which defines man's originary skill or ability—which Hölderlin will translate with the German *Geschick*, virtuosity and destiny (and we are aware of the speculative fortune that this word will have). Man, in other words, is originarily a being of *tekhnē*, in the sense of *know-how*. This is moreover what allows Rousseau to simultaneously refute Hobbes's thesis (man is a bellicose animal) and

Montesquieu's, confirmed by Cumberland and Pufendorf (man is a fearful animal). The savage man is neither aggressive nor afraid, for the good reason that "living dispersed amongst the animals and early finding himself in the position of having to measure himself against them, soon makes the comparison and, feeling that he surpasses them in skill more than they do him in strength, learns to fear them no more" (DI 143). But let us note well: He *learns* to fear them no more.

We must in fact suppose, at this first (instrumental) stage of *tekhnē*, an originary faculty of *comparison*. And this is nothing other—if we think of Aristotle's *Poetics* (22, 1459a) but also of *Problemata* XXX, 12—than the metaphorical faculty (*to metaphorikon einai*) as the originary theoretical faculty (the faculty of seeing likeness [*le semblable*], and therefore of distinguishing difference: *to gar eu metaphorein to to homoion theōrein estin*) and as the sign of a natural gift or of genius, *euphuia* (*ingenium*). *Tekhnē*, in the sense of the tropic or polytropic art, is man's genius, his naturally a-natural or super-natural gift, since it "supplements" the defect or lack of instinct. Man is a tropic animal—yet another formulation of the founding oxymoron, which will not be without consequences, moreover, with regard to the figural origin of language and the inaugural "transport" of sociality (in particular in the *Essay on the Origin of Languages*).

But if man is indeed so—and this is the other analysis that Rousseau carries out, still in line with Aristotle—it is first of all by virtue of the fact that man is a mimetic animal. This is the second stage, that is, a stage even more primitive than *tekhnē*. In the *agōn* that opposes him not to other men, as in Hobbes, but to the animals—this *agōn* is the originary *agōn*, which means that the origin is agonal (neither Hegel nor Heidegger will forget this)—man supplements his defect or lack of instinct through his genius for imitation—which is, in fact, the very primary condition of his sur-vival (of his metaphysical life):

> The Earth, abandoned to its natural fertility and covered by immense forests which no Axe ever mutilated, at every step offers Storage and shelter to the animals or every species. Men, dispersed among them, observe, imitate their industry, and so raise themselves to the level of the Beasts' instinct, with this advantage, that each species has but its own instinct, while man, perhaps having none that belongs to him, appropriates them all, feeds indifferently on most of the various foods which the other animals divide among themselves, and as a result finds his subsistence more easily than can any one of them. (DI 142)

What is surprising here is not so much that Rousseau would still closely follow the *Poetics* (whether he knows it or not), in particular the famous opening of chapter IV (1448b) where Aristotle defines man as *mimētēs phusei* and deduces from this definition, by means of pleasure or joy—Rousseau says *jouissance*, "enjoyment"[2]—the faculty of *manthanein* and of *theōrein*. The tropic faculty, then. What is surprising is that this definition is *the very definition of the actor* which Rousseau—in response to arguments that he knows well and which will indeed resurface against him, much later, in Diderot's *Paradox*—is the first to make his own, in the *Letter to M. d'Alembert on the Theater*, but obviously in order to condemn the theater, and to do so by repeating Plato (if not the church fathers): the actor, possessing no proper character, is apt (*propre*) to appropriate all characters.[3] He is "the man without qualities" (or more exactly "without properties"), as Musil says.

Man is therefore, originarily, an actor. Such is, at bottom, his advantageous organization and what makes him into more (which is to say less) than "an ingenious machine to which nature has given senses in order to wind itself up and, to a point, protect itself against everything that tends to destroy it" (DI 148). We are still in Aristotle: it is because man is a naturally unfinished being that the art in him—mimetism, that is, *tekhnē mimētikē*—achieves and completes what nature was not able to operate (*oeuvrer*). Of course Rousseau translates this intuition in terms of freedom and perfectibility: "I perceive precisely the same thing in the human machine, with this difference that Nature alone does everything in the *operations* of the Beast, whereas man contributes to his operations in his capacity as a free agent" (DI 148, my emphasis). But this freedom—or, on the following page, this "faculty of perfecting oneself"—consists entirely of this gift of being able to be *everything* through the fact of being *nothing*. In other words, knowing how to *play*.[4]

Nothing forbids us, then, from thinking that the state of nature is a theater or, more exactly, that a *primal scene* accounts for or explains the denaturing of man, meaning his obligated entry—or his birth—into history and culture: into the *play* (*jeu*) of history and culture.

This scene is perfectly identifiable; and we know that such a scene will return regularly, in one form or another.[5] It is indeed primal. It precedes, by far, the installation of the reign of freedom and the exercise of perfectibility that, in reality, suppose it.

This takes place in the preface: Rousseau has just rejected the idea of natural Law, which is to say the very subject that had been proposed to him. He then says this:

> Hence, disregarding all the scientific books that only teach us to see men as they have made themselves, and meditating on the first and simplest operations of the human Soul, I believe I perceive in it two principles prior to reason, of which one interests us intensely in our well-being and our self-preservation, and the other inspires in us a natural repugnance at seeing any sentient Being, and especially any being like ourselves, perish or suffer. It is from the association and combination which our mind is capable of making between these two Principles, without it being necessary to introduce into it that of sociability, that all the rules of natural right seem to me to flow; rules which reason

is subsequently forced to reestablish on different foundations when, by its successive developments, it has succeeded in smothering nature. (DI 132–133)

Jean Starobinski is not wrong in thinking that one finds here the matrix of the entire dialectical thought of history, which is to say the very principle of historicity, as it will develop beginning with Kant: from the perspective of the problematic of natural rights, it is clearly indicated that, once the state of nature is lost, it is up to reason or culture, which has negated it, to "reestablish [it] on other foundations" and thus to permit what Kant will postulate as "a reconciliation of *nature* and *culture* by the intermediary of 'practical reason.'" Starobinski adds, moreover, that "according to Rousseau, society's task is to preserve what it has negated," which offers, he says, "a striking example of what Hegel will name *Aufhebung*."[6] This is undeniable. But what Starobinski does not notice here—nor does anyone else, to my knowledge—is the strangely familiar character of the principial (prerational and presocial) antinomy on which Rousseau bases himself: of the "first and simplest *operations* [my emphasis again] of the Human Soul," one of which, he specifies, "interests us intensely in our well-being and our self-preservation, and the other inspires in us a natural repugnance at seeing any sentient Being, and especially any being like ourselves, perish or suffer."

The second of these operations, of which Rousseau will develop a broad analysis, is that of pity, this pity that, against Hobbes and thanks to Mandeville—despite his being "the most extreme Detractor of human virtues"—Rousseau considers as "the only Natural virtue": "a disposition suited to beings as weak and as subject to so many ills as we are; a virtue all the more universal and useful to man as it precedes the exercise of all reflection in him, and so Natural that the Beasts themselves sometimes show evident signs of it" (DI 160). The first, for its part, which is not a virtue (and which it is pity's function, precisely, to "moderate") is self-love (*l'amour de soi*), which Rousseau carefully distinguishes from vanity (*l'amour-propre*), its social graft (note XV, DI 226), and defines as "a natural sentiment which inclines every animal to attend to its self-preservation."

Just as pity poses hardly any problem—even if Rousseau, in significant fashion, will no doubt shrink back from his own discovery, which is nothing less than that of the originarity of transport and of identification, that is, of the imagination (which in sum is already, as we are beginning to see, the transcendental itself);[7] likewise self-love—the instinct for preservation, as it precisely must not be called—remains enigmatic: the fact is that Rousseau, still against Hobbes and Montesquieu, does not want to refer it directly to fear, and therefore to unkindness or hate, even if he cannot avoid linking it to a primal agonistic and, consequently, to the perception of a danger: "Self-preservation being almost his only care, his most developed faculties must be those that primarily serve in attack and defense, either in order to overcome his prey or to guard against becoming another animal's prey" (DI 147). Self-love, Rousseau must indeed recognize, supposes the fear of perishing; and this is indeed why, moreover, it is inseparable from sympathetic projection or identification, which supposes, in fact, the *same* fear.[8]

Fear and pity, then. You will have recognized here the two *pathemata* that, according to Aristotle, tragedy functions to *kathairein*, to purify or to purge. (Let us admit, provisionally, these two translations, without for the moment attempting to distinguish them.) I have elsewhere offered the hypothesis that the functional theory of tragedy is properly political, and that Aristotle places within the principle of the tragic effect the two transcendental (and antinomical) affects of sociality: the affect of *association* or of connection (pity) and that of *dissociation* or disconnection (fear). And it is the task of politics, and of the political art par excellence (which is to say also politics as art, which is not at all a separate issue), to regulate or to "moderate" the possible excess of these two affects: whether it be a war of all against all, or communal fusion, both equally disastrous. (But it is likewise Rousseau who allows the formulation of this hypothesis.[9] Against Plato, in this case, who sees in pity and fear only weaknesses of the citizen-soldier, or the soldier-citizen: therefore a danger for the militarized State.)

The *origin* then presupposes, indeed, a *representation*: *mimēsis* or *Darstellung*.

I have spoken of a *primal scene* or an *originary theater*. For it is striking to see the extent to which a theatrical metaphorics governs all of Rousseau's analyses.

In the case of pity, it is all too evident. Everything is based on the principle that "commiseration will be all the more energetic in proportion as the *Onlooking animal* [*l'animal Spectateur*] identifies more intimately with the suffering animal" (DI 162, my emphasis); and we easily see that Rousseau's entire description authorizes itself in fact on the basis of the enigma—or the paradox—of the tragic effect. The description opens with the following major argument: "Such is the pure movement of Nature prior to all reflection: such is the force of natural pity which the most depraved morals still have difficulty destroying, since in our theaters one daily sees being moved and weeping at the miseries of some unfortunate person, people who, if they were in the Tyrant's place, would only increase their enemy's torments" (DI 161). Rousseau is in fact so attached to this argument that in a late addition he reiterates word for word a passage from the *Letter to d'Alembert*, inspired by Plutarch and Montaigne: "like bloodthirsty Sulla, so sensitive to ills which he had not caused, or that Alexander of Pherae who dared not attend the performance of a single tragedy for fear that he might be seen to moan with Andromache and Priam, but who listened without emotion to the cries of so many citizens daily being murdered on his orders" (DI 161). I will return to this "insert" in a moment.

But in the case of self-love, things are no less clear, and we find again the same metaphorics. For example, from the start of the discussion of Hobbes and Montesquieu, regarding fear: "That may be so with regard to the objects he does not know, and I do not doubt that he is frightened by all new *Sights* [Spectacles] that present themselves to him when he cannot tell whether to expect Physical good or evil from them, or when he cannot compare his strength with the dangers he runs" (DI 143, my emphasis). Or again in note XV, concerning the distinction between self-love and pride: "I say that in our primitive state, in the genuine state of nature, Vanity does not exist; For, since every individual human being views himself *as the only Spectator* to observe him, as the only being in the universe to take any interest in him, as the only judge of his own merit, it is not possible that a sentiment which originates in comparisons he is not capable of making, could spring up in his soul" (DI 226, my emphasis).

These texts speak for themselves. I do not see it as useful, here, to paraphrase them.

But I would like, at this point, to suspend things for a moment.

Onto-technology, as Rousseau founds it, thus opening the possibility of a thought of historicity, therefore supposes a *theater*. Existence is historical ("historial") insofar as man plays it, that is, imagines it, if it is true—and it is incontestably true—that *imago* and *imitatio* (*mimēsis*) belong to the same semantic field. The scene is, in fact, primal.

This is what Hölderlin very precisely retained from Rousseau when he worked out his interpretation of history—meaning: of the history of art, of the relationship between *phusis* and *tekhnē*, nature and culture, "aorgic" and "organic" (but all history is perhaps fundamentally, since Rousseau, a history of art)—on the basis of Sophocles' tragedies *Antigone* and *Oedipus*, the one emblematic of ancient tragedy, the other of modern tragedy.[10] And it is also, very precisely, what Heidegger does not want to hear about: beyond the fact that he does not offer the least commentary on what are known as Hölderlin's "theoretical" texts on theater and tragedy (*The Ground of Empedocles*, and the *Remarks* on the translations of Sophocles[11]), we recall his lapidary declaration, in the 1936 lectures on "The Origin of the Work of Art," in which, repeating Hegel, he lays out an entire onto-theology of art and, from there, an aesthetico-political theology: tragedy, he says in substance, the poetic tragic work, is a question neither of execution nor of staging, and therefore has nothing to do, if we dare say, with the theater; it is the site of the struggle or combat (*Kampf* or *Streit*: *polemos*) between ancient and new gods.

Without a doubt, and aside from the blindness already indicated—which is immense—the philosophical contempt displayed toward Rousseau is not without some basis. I have evoked, taking my inspiration in fact from the Heideggerian reading of Kant and from his interpretation, precisely, of the transcendental schematism (therefore, of the *transcendental imagination*), Rousseau's *shrinking back*. This is nowhere more manifest than when—at a point of extreme condensation—Rousseau collides directly with two aporetic difficulties which, linked together and treated on the basis of the existential analytic and fundamental ontology, will provide the entire resource for the "step back" in the metaphysics of the *animal rationale* and of the *zōon logon ekhōn*.

The first difficulty—and there is nothing surprising in this—is related to fear. As part of a genealogy of the passions, Rousseau notes that savage man, "deprived of every sort of enlightenment," experiences only the passions that derive from "the simple impulsion of Nature." He then adds (and here the empiricist evasion is patent): "his desires do not exceed his Physical needs; the only goods he knows in the Universe are food, a female, and rest; the only evils he fears are pain, and hunger; I say pain, and not death; for an animal will never know what it is to die, and the knowledge of death and of its terrors was one of man's first acquisitions on moving away from the animal condition" (DI 150).

The second difficulty, for its part, is very famous; it overdetermines—and no doubt blocks in certain ways— the whole thought of Rousseau up to the *Social Contract*; it appears in this formula of renunciation that will burden the vain attempt of the *Essay on the Origin of Languages*: "As for me, frightened by the increasing difficulties, and convinced of the almost demonstrated impossibility that Languages could have arisen and been established by purely human means, I leave to anyone who wishes to undertake it, the discussion of this difficult Problem: which was the more necessary, an already united Society for the institution of Languages, or already invented Languages for the establishment of Society?" (DI 157–158).

It therefore appears that in Rousseau we do not find the determination—assuredly tragic—of the essence of man as "the mortal possessing speech (or language, or even *langue*: *die Sprache*)," this formula preceding every ontological one—let us give it this much credit—that punctuates Heidegger's last teachings. This would also be the secret of Rousseau's "liberalism," and the manifestation of his philosophical insufficiency. Unless—but this would require an entirely different demonstration—the mortal having language, or even *langue*, were already detectable in Rousseau's work: in which case, programmed politics, up to Heidegger's era, would perhaps be Terror . . . by which I mean: politics founded on the *ordeal* (*épreuve*), in every sense, of death.[12] But this lapidary allusion is worth no more than it is worth (and it would be good, one day, to examine *seriously* what Jacobin politics, and revolutionary statism in general, owe in the end to Rousseau).

More important, at the point where we find ourselves, is in reality the task of asking ourselves what Rousseau truly means by *acquisition* when he says "the knowledge of death and of its terrors was one of man's first acquisitions on moving away [*en s'éloignant*] from the animal condition" (DI 150). To put it another way: what does "moving away" or *distancing* (*éloignement*) mean? What, here, are the nature, the measure, or the commensurability of distance? Or of the "interval," as Rousseau says? This is the whole question of the hiatus, or the abyss, between nature and culture: of the *caesura* of the origin. It is, in consequence, the whole question of the *manthanein*, in Aristotle's sense (to learn, to acquire): of *mimetic mathematics*, if we can thus condense the translation of the beginning of chapter IV of the *Poetics*. And finally, the entire question of the preposition *meta*: meta-physics or meta-phor, in any case *trans-port*. How to conceive of the originary *ek-stasis*, or of the origin—the *Ur-sprung*, the "leap," the originary "surging forth"—the incommensurable *dis-stancing* (*Ent-fernung*) of the origin? The *de-propriation* which alone grants access to the *proper*, to speak Hölderlin's language? In short, *transcendental negativity*?

Heidegger, if he had wished, could have made himself attentive to Rousseau's *thought*. He manifestly *refused*. But in thus refusing to assign him a place in the history and destiny of philosophy—and therefore, inextricably, of "poetry"—he perhaps missed this *turning* of thought where, under the question of the origin of politics, it is the origin of thought (of the meta-physical as such) that suddenly rises to the level of philosophical questioning. There was in Rousseau's thought, assuredly in an obscure manner, everything needed to detect what, in fact, Cassirer or "liberal thought" were unable to detect in it (but that Kant, Hölderlin, and Hegel, for their part, had clearly perceived): namely that the origin or the possibility of metaphysics is nothing other than meta-physics *as* origin, and that such is the sense of what I call here, awkwardly, Rousseau's onto-technology.

Heidegger's "slip-up"—and it was literally that—was political.[13] Granted. But this means, in all simplicity, that it was *philosophical*. It is useless, and disastrous, to mask this obvious fact. The whole question remains: what exactly does Heidegger dread in Rousseau's work? An inadequate conception of "nature"? That is the official version, meaning *his* version. It unfortunately implies that he never for a moment attempted to read him; which, at the same time, is hardly likely. Could it be the thought—submerged but accessible—of "originary theatricality," or of originary *mimēsis*? That would surely be more likely here, even if, in an irreducible paradox, it is none other than Heidegger himself who at bottom authorizes the intuition of such a thought. The disagreement would bear in this case on the originarity of the *concept* of *mimēsis*, regarding which Heidegger, as we know, is no more satisfied than he is with the concept of *natura*. The disagreement bears, then, in short, on *theater*—for which Heidegger maintained a tenacious hatred and contempt.

But so did Rousseau . . . in whose work, as is well known, hatred and contempt for the theater are even more openly *declared* and explicitly *claimed*. What, then, is involved here?

It is impossible, on this point, to leave the question in suspense.

PART TWO

Anterior Theater

1

The attempt to find in Rousseau's work *another thought* of the theater, different from the one that he uses to condemn it irrevocably, would appear to be a senseless undertaking, and, as such, doomed to failure; or else, even worse, it gives rise to all sorts of subtle and fabricated, arbitrary and fallacious elaborations: "vain sophisms," as he would have said, though he liked nothing so much as "paradoxes." To be sure, no one ignores the fact that Rousseau was *also* a "man of the theater": that he wrote for the theater, that he was met with some success, and would have gladly made it his career; that he regularly frequented, at least for a certain time, the theaters of Paris and Venice, and that he had, as in everything, an excellent knowledge of the repertoire, both classic and modern, and possessed a vast culture on the subject of theatrical poetry. But after all, the "doctrine" is there; and there is not the least bit of ambiguity in it: as he said and repeated, beginning in the first *Discourse*, or even in the preface to *Narcissus*, the theater, as indeed literature in general, is a social and political "poison." It is, literally and in every sense, the *opium of the people*. There is nothing in the least that would be able to "save" it.

Everything has been said about this condemnation; it would seem useless to go back over it.

I will nevertheless stubbornly insist on the question. And I set out from the following, which I previously noted only in passing: How is it that Rousseau felt the need, at the time of the preparation of a new edition of the second *Discourse* (which, in truth, did not appear until after his death, in the Moultou and Du Peyrou edition), to include in his analysis of "natural" pity, whose absolutely decisive importance one can hardly dispute, the passage from the *Letter to d'Alembert* that justified his questioning of the claimed "moral effect" of theater in general, and of tragedy in particular? Rousseau had written, as we remember: "Such is the pure movement of Nature prior to all reflection: such is the force of natural pity which the most depraved morals still have difficulty destroying, since in our theaters one daily sees being moved and weeping at the miseries of some unfortunate person, people who, if they were in the Tyrant's place, would only increase their enemy's torments" (DI 161). He was quite insistent, then, on the insertion at this very point of these few lines from the *Letter*, which in fact come down from Plutarch and Montaigne, the latter recopying the former, etc: "like bloodthirsty Sulla, so sensitive to ills which he had not caused, or that Alexander of Pherae who dared not attend the performance of a single tragedy for fear that he might be seen to moan with Andromache and Priam [Montaigne had written: "Hecuba and Andromache"—L.-L.], but who listened without emotion to the cries of so many citizens daily being murdered on his orders" (DI 161).[1]

The question, then, is very simple: What justifies, here, this addition or this belated "insert"?

And the answer, consequently, is no less simple: the completely Aristotelian overdetermination of the originary problematic of pity. As well as that of fear, in fact, though this is less obvious.

This is obviously what we must attempt to demonstrate.

Let us start again from the *Letter*.

In what context exactly had Rousseau first recalled these two anecdotes, or these two "examples"? In the context, as we well know, of the discussion of Aristotle that forms practically, through various angles of attack, the entire object of the text. More precisely, at issue there was a (violent) contestation of the too famous, or too enigmatic, *katharsis*: the beneficial effect, as one said at the time, or the "moral" or therapeutic function of the theatrical representation of the "passions." Like anyone critically examining the theater, during the "classical" period at any rate, Rousseau had therefore undertaken to reread the *Poetics*, and of course its chapter VI, infelicitously dissociated, as common practice dictated, from the opening of chapter IV, meaning from the major proposition concerning the *mimetic effect*, without which the doctrine of *katharsis* remains incomprehensible.

The usual commentary of the *Letter* holds that, within the economy of the text, the discussion of Aristotle is not central, but incidental, lateral, laboriously *obligated*: It was very necessary, in that age, to make it known that one properly knew the Authority, who, on this subject, was unique. Moreover, Rousseau quotes Aristotle only secondhand (in Latin . . .); he refers in reality only to the poeticians of his time, or of the previous century (Crébillion, for example, or Du Bos, but he has clearly read the prefaces and essays of Corneille, Racine, Voltaire, and several others); his professed contempt regarding Aristotle's indulgent attitude toward tragedy is in proportion to the hate (or fear)—openly Platonist— which he feels for the *fact* of the theater, regardless of whether tragedy or comedy (*The Misanthrope* . . . his likeness, his brother). No doubt. But this "characterization" is rather cursory. This is not at all how things happen in the *Letter*; and it is necessary, after all, to look a little more closely.

Aristotle does not come up just incidentally, nor, even less, "for the record." He is present from the start, or almost.

We must take Rousseau at his word. As always, in fact. His critique of the theater owes nothing to the Church Fathers,[2] despite their not entirely well-founded reputation for having simply transmitted the Platonic argument. His critique owes nothing, either, despite certain more solid appearances, to the Calvinist hatred for "comedy," "amusements," and spectacles. In doctrinal matters, Rousseau also knows what he is saying, as shown, in fact, by the long initial defense of the Geneva pastorate—which is not merely a *captatio benevolentiae* for his compatriots' benefit—against the accusation, smugly repeated and treacherously amplified by d'Alembert, of a "Socinian" heresy.[3] No, if Rousseau condemns the theater and vigorously excludes its eventual official installation in Geneva—in the "Republic of Geneva"—it is for fundamentally philosophical reasons. And, consequently, political ones. This is why his *inspiration* is rigorously Platonist. And we know, moreover, that initially Rousseau planned to attach to his reply a "translation" (adaptation or paraphrase) of the "various places where Plato treats theatrical imitation," composed almost exclusively, in fact, of passages from book X of *The Republic*.[4]

However, he did not in fact attach this "piece." And for reasons that are anything but inessential, as he will himself admit, without quite saying so, when it is published separately in 1764.[5] The fact is that, in reality, this reminder of the conclusive theses of *The Republic*—including, here and there, a few borrowings from the *Gorgias* or the *Laws*, with *one exception*, to which I will return in a moment—deals relatively little with the theater as such. The clearest proof of this is the absence, practically, of any reference to books II and III of *The*

Republic, precisely where we see develop, in the detailed and irrevocable manner of which we are aware, the entire Platonic critique of tragedy, notably founded on the exclusion of its specific mode of representation or enunciation, that is, on the condemnation, including in the epic poem (Homer), of the "mimetic" *lexis*, or, if you prefer, of the dialogic mode, where the author does not speak in his own name, but makes "persons" speak. *On Theatrical Imitation* is a treatise on imitation in general, one that proceeds from the distinction between "usage," "fabrication," and "imitation" and is grounded on the privileged paradigms of "making" (*poiein*), in this case, of architecture (the example of the three temples is substituted for that of the three beds in *The Republic*), and of painting. Certainly, poetry is the main enemy; but as in Plato's work, in large part, it is Homer who is the first target, the "leader" of the tragedians, who claims to speak of everything without truly knowing anything and who is only illusorily "the teacher [*instituteur*] of Greece," when in fact, unlike a Lycurgus, a Charondas, a Minos, or a Solon, he never in reality founded or instituted anything, and was in no way ever a legislator. Moreover, again as in Plato's work, the only art allowed is state poetry—which we might well call, after all, the "theologico-political genre":

> But always consider that the Hymns in honor of the Gods and the praises of great men are the sole type of Poetry which should be admitted into the Republic,

and that, if it once allows within it that imitative Muse which charms us and deceives us by the sweetness of its accents, men's actions will soon no longer have as their object either the law or good and beautiful things, but pain and sensual pleasure; aroused passions will dominate instead of reason; the Citizens will no longer be virtuous and just men, always subject to duty and to equity, but sensitive and weak men who will do good or evil indifferently according as they are led by their inclination. (TI 349)

This does not mean that it is not at all a question of theater, particularly of tragedy. But theater is here considered solely from the point of view of what Plato called *logos* (the "content" or statement) in opposition to *lexis*, that is, as a vehicle for fallacious "myths" or fabricated fables, and an incitement, through its power of mimetic contagion (which for its part remains unanalyzed), to ethically and politically inadmissible behaviors: dangerous, vile, indulgent, unworthy, atrocious, voluptuous (etc.) actions, which stem from "the most feeble part of the soul." In other words, what is in question here is *pathos*. Or if you prefer, the theater is fundamentally pathological, and, as a consequence, pathogenic. Hence this double conclusion, which, for its part, is perhaps not exclusively Platonic:

Finally, never forget that by banishing Dramas and Theatrical Pieces from our State, we are not following a barbarous obstinacy and do not at all scorn the beauties of the art, but we prefer to them the immortal beauties that result from the harmony of the soul and from the concord of its faculties.[6]

Let us do still more. In order to protect ourselves from all partiality and to grant nothing to that ancient discord that reigns between the Philosophers and the Poets, let us not take from Poetry and from imitation anything they may allege in their defense, nor from ourselves the innocent pleasures they can procure for us. . . . In sometimes lending our ears to Poetry, we will prevent our hearts from being imposed upon by it and we will not allow it to trouble order and freedom, either in the interior Republic of the soul or in that of human society. (TI 349–50)

There remains, nevertheless, the exception to which I referred a moment ago: the unique place where Rousseau is openly inspired by a passage drawn from book III of *The Republic*. It is not at all by chance that it is a question here, in the last analysis, of *pity*.

Rousseau begins from this observation—taken in this case from book X, as we have just learned—that it is from the "sensitive and weak part [of the soul] that the touching and varied imitations seen on the stage are drawn." He has just evoked "mourning, tears, despair, moans." And he adds: "The man who is firm, prudent, and always like himself is not so easy to imitate, and, even if he were, the imitation, being less varied, would not be as pleasant to the Vulgar." (As we know, the argument is one that in the *Letter* is aimed at *The Misanthrope*.) Then he continues directly, or nearly so; and I allow myself to emphasize, for reasons already known or that will emerge later, two of the concepts that this declaration advances. Here is where the quasi-quotation of book III begins:

> never does the human heart *identify* with objects that it feels are absolutely foreign to it. In addition, the skillful Poet, the Poet who knows the art of succeeding, seeking to please the People and vulgar men, is quite wary of offering them the sublime image of a heart that is master of itself, that hears only the voice of wisdom; but he charms the spectators by characters who are always in *contradiction*, who want and do not want, who make the Theaters ring with cries and moans, who force us to pity them, even when they do their duty, and to think virtue is a sad thing since it makes its friends so miserable. (TI 346–347, my emphasis)

There follows a long development that places book III in communication with book X and culminates, quite logically, with the "conflict of the faculties" and the "dissensions . . . into the Republic of the soul" (TI 347), comparable to those of the Republic itself, which is to say equally harmful by the very fact of the "inversion," here of "healthy opinions," there of the relationship of "the good to the bad" or of "the true leaders to the rebels." No surprise, then, that it should be essentially (false) pity—artificial pity provoked by imitation—

that is incriminated in the end, in terms that are nearly identical to those we find in the *Letter*:

> Are these not very useful Spectacles rather than those which we would blush to imitate, and wherein we are interested in the weaknesses from which we take such trouble to protect ourselves in our own calamities? The most noble faculty of the soul, thus losing the power and the empire over itself, grows accustomed to bend under the law of the passions; it no longer re-presses our tears and our cries; it delivers us over to our *tenderness* for objects which are foreign to us; and under the pretext of *commiseration* for chimerical misfortunes, far from being indignant that a virtuous man abandons himself to excessive grieving, far from preventing us from applauding his degradation, it lets us applaud ourselves for the *pity* which it inspires in us; it is a pleasure we believe we have gained without weakness and taste without remorse. (TI 348, my emphasis)

It is indeed *katharsis*, then, that Rousseau is attacking and, in this context at the very least, which is to say the "Platonic" context, the *katharsis* of pity. As a consequence, he is essentially taking aim at Aristotle; and this is perhaps the reason why the *Letter*, which is basically addressed to the latter, albeit indirectly, thanks to the succession of classical French poeticians, had no need to repeat the Platonic argument in its entirety. It was enough for Rousseau to base his argument, implicitly, on what in Plato authorizes and supports the condemnation of the theater in order, by the same token, to take aim at the *Poetics* or its successors, viewed for at least two centuries as the anti-Platonist manifesto par excellence on the subject of "aesthetics." In these conditions, it is not at all aberrant to consider that Aristotle is indeed present in the *Letter* from the start, and that d'Alembert, having had the misfortune of implicating Geneva, was merely a stand-in.

Three indisputable facts confirm this.

There is first of all the moment when, having barely begun the discussion of the theater, Rousseau, adept as he is in this type of critical exercise, accumulates or enumerates the multiple questions that to his mind d'Alembert's article suggests—which is to say, in sum, the questions that d'Alembert did not even ask himself or showed himself unable to formulate. At this point everything converges on the single "problem" of the "true effects of the theater." After expressing indignation at d'Alembert for having one day appeared as "the first Philosopher who has ever encouraged a free people, a small city, and a poor State to burden itself with a public Theater" (LA 15) (and this is, as we know, one of the major political arguments of the *Letter*), Rousseau forcefully attacks:

How many questions I find to discuss in what you appear to have settled! Whether the Theatre is good or bad in itself? Whether it can be united with morals?

Whether it is in conformity with republican austerity? Whether it ought to be tolerated in a little city? Whether the Actor's profession can be a decent one? Whether Actresses can be as well behaved as other women? Whether good laws suffice for repressing the abuses? Whether these laws can be well observed? etc. Everything is still problematic concerning the real effects of the Theater; for, since the disputes that it occasions are solely between the Men of the Church and the Men of the world, each side views the problem only through its prejudices. Here, Sir, are studies that would not be unworthy of your pen. (LA 261)

We find ourselves, consequently, and from the beginning, at the center of the conflict between Aristotle and Plato, which must be urgently reexamined and submitted to authentic philosophers, and not abandoned to subordinate quarrels between the Church and the World. These "real effects of the Theater" will be the question of the *Letter*; and we will hardly be surprised to see this questioning brought to bear upon the *Poetics* and its lesson, even if only half glimpsed, concerning the *truth* of the theater.

In the second place—the repercussion is immediate— having reminded us that since spectacles[7] are "made for the people," they can include "an infinity of types" (according to the "diversity of morals, temperaments, and characters," or the "diverse tastes of nations": an unsurprising historicist thesis), that only "pleasure" and not "utility" determines them, and that "the Stage, in general" (for there is indeed, despite everything, an essence of the theater) "is a tableau of the human passions, the original of which lies in every heart," Rousseau hammers home the point that reason alone could be capable of correcting the passions, but that, precisely, "it is only reason that is good for nothing on the Stage": "A man without passions or who always mastered them could not attract anyone. And it has already been observed that a Stoic in Tragedy would be an insufferable figure. In Comedy he would, at most, cause laughter" (LA 264).[8] And a few pages later, although here it is *katharsis* which is explicitly interrogated (I will return to this point), he adds: "Do we not know that all the passions are sisters and that one alone suffices for arousing a thousand, and that to combat one by the other is only the way to make the heart more sensitive to them all? The only instrument which serves to purge them is reason, and I have already said that reason has no effect in theater" (LA 265).

There remains finally everything that has to do with the openly Platonist politico-philosophical (and therefore ethical) preferences, which we know are the very opposite of Aristotle's conception of the *bios politikos*: the economy or the drastic management of work hours and the quasi-exclusion of leisure and idleness;[9] the privileging of the proper and of ipseity, which brings with it the famous condemnation—taken, for its part, from *Republic III*—of the (false) profession of actor;[10] and, on the horizon, in lieu of State Poetry, the "civic festival," greatly criticized and misunderstood (notably by the reactionary or "liberal" historians of the French Revolution), and which is probably the final attempt to force or break through what Jacques Derrida once called "the closure of representation": the very division of the spectacle, the separation of the "audience" and the "stage," the viewer and the viewed; or to envisage the utopia of a pure spectacle, a spectacle without "spectacle," reduced to the sole self-representation of the people in the joy of love and fraternity: communion itself, in a Spartan mode (as is required), or the felicitous realization of the community as a living work of art.[11]

At least two conditions are necessary in order to arrive at this result, conditions that are, furthermore, inextricably linked but that Rousseau separates from each other, abusively, because at bottom he did not truly read the *Poetics*. What I mean by this is quite simply that the critique of *katharsis*, which in the end makes up the entire object of the *Letter*, is only possible, in the terms under which Rousseau carries it out, if one misunderstands the function that Aristotle attributes to *mimēsis*.

A critique of *katharsis* on the basis of the Platonic conception of *mimēsis* does not present the least difficulty: nothing is more *facile*, in every sense of the term. It suffices to confine *mimēsis* within the boundaries of the "passions" or the carefully delineated (and separate) field of "sensibility," and to deny it any intelligence or any "theoretical" function. The well-known depreciation (simple "imitation" or reproduction, copy or copy of a copy, simulacrum or pretense, "aping," as the tradition elegantly puts it) is but a consequence of this. But Aristotle does not speak at all in these terms: *mimēsis* gives rise to thought. If it is not *thought* itself or *thinking* that it gives rise to, it is at least that which makes them possible. It offers the condition for learning (*mathein*) and for seeing (*theōrein*), that is, for recognition of the same or of likeness (the singular thing itself, *the same*[12]). Its function—*just like* that of metaphor or comparison—is *mathematical* and *theoretical*. And that, moreover, is the reason for the joy (*kharis*), or for the "enjoyment [*jouissance*]" as Rousseau says, that it provokes, and for the pleasure (*hēdonē*) that accompanies it, all of which is innate, natural (naive or native): properly human.

Is it really necessary to quote this passage, yet again?

Representation comes naturally to human beings from childhood, and so does the universal pleasure [*to khairen*] in representations [*mimeisthai*]. Indeed, this marks off humans from other animals: man is prone to representation beyond all others, and learns his earliest lessons [*mathēseis*] through representation. . . . The further explanation of this is that learning is delightful [*manthanein . . . hēdiston*] not only to philosophers but to ordinary people as well. . . . That is why people like seeing images, because as they look [*theōrountas* (from *theōrein*)] at them they understand [*manthanein*] and work out [*sullogizesthai*] what each thing is [*ti hekaston*], for example, "that is so-and-so." (*Poetics*, 1448b)[13]

As is well known, this analysis *also* bears the mark of a certain "empiricism": the proof or the sign (*sēmeion*) of this joy or this pleasure that we find in representations, says Aristotle, are found in "practical experience," in the facts (*epi tōn ergōn*). And these facts are images or icons. Aristotle thinks *first* of painting here: "even when things are painful to look upon—corpses, for instance, or the shapes of the most revolting animals—we take pleasure in viewing highly realistic images of them." Likewise, having mentioned the pleasure of recognition ("that is so and so"), he adds: "Whereas, if one is unacquainted with the subject, one's pleasure will not be in the representation, but in the technique or the color or some other element." But these "empirical" examples, the first one at least, have no end other than indicating in advance the very strange "alchemy" of *katharsis*: the transmutation of pain (*lupē*) into pleasure. Or, to put it more brutally (and in anticipation), of *negative* into *positive*. And all things being equal, they are to "transcendental mimetology" in a way what the "mirror stage" is to a certain onto-psychology: the experimental verification, or if you prefer the verification at the level of existence itself, of an irrecusable a priori, of a condition of existence as such. In this sense, the "jubilation" at the *mimēme* is indeed a *sign*.

Empiricism or not, it matters little after all. Rousseau, at any rate, did not *read* this text, and was doubtless unable to read it. It is difficult in any case to see what, in the ancient and especially Roman tradition (the Horatian moralization, for example, of the poetic function)— or in the "modern" tradition, drawn from the Latin translation of Averroes' commentary, or from the direct translation, into Latin, of the text of the *Poetics* by William of Moerbeke, in the thirteenth century, but truly operative beginning in the Italian Renaissance[14]— could have put him on another path and made him think (or repeat) anything other than: Art imitates nature, imitation is part of the imaginary (*imago*, or even "*ut pictura poesis*"), nature (in "literature" and in the theater) consists of "characters" and human passions. Certainly not French classicism, which hardly freed itself, on this subject, from the Cinquecento. To borrow Alain Badiou's lexicon, nowhere in the tradition is the Mimeme capable of a Matheme, except as a moral *lesson*; and in reality this comes close to invalidating every Poem.

We already know the result: "the Stage, in general, is a tableau of the human passions, the original of which lies in every heart."

Under this second condition, how could *katharsis* be comprehensible?

Rousseau is the first (and this is his fundamental honesty) to admit that he does not know: "I know that the Poetics of the Theater claims to . . . purge the passions in exciting them. But I have difficulty understanding this rule. Is it possible that in order to become temperate and prudent we must begin by being intemperate and mad?" (LA 265).[15] He conceives even less the aforementioned rule in that, in conformity with the "classics," he commits at least four errors regarding Aristotle's text. The very famous statement of Aristotle says the following:

> Tragedy is a representation of an action of a superior kind—grand, and complete in itself—presented in embellished language, in distinct forms in different parts, performed by actors rather than told by a narrator, effecting, through pity and fear, the purification of such emotions. (*Poetics*, 1449b)

The four errors, always the same, are well known:

1. Tragedy, if not "the Stage, in general," is the representation of an *action*, not of the "passions"; it is even, more literally, representation of action (*mimēsis praxeōs*): whence the relative subordination, in Aristotle's work, of the "character" (*ethos*) of those carrying out the actions, of the characters who act on stage (*prattontes*), in relation to the *drama*, properly speaking, or to the *muthos* "in act" (to the story or the "fable," as Brecht says, insofar as it is *mise en scène*, or "presented").

2. The "passions," if there are passions, are not *the* passions in general; at the very most, "fear and pity" (or affects of a similar kind), if at least, which is far from certain, the *di'eleou kai phobou* supposes a *dia mimeseōs*

eleou kai phobou [through the *mimēsis* of fear and pity], which is to say that one *represents* "fear and fright" *on stage*: the question here is to know what is the exact *means* of *katharsis*: the awakening, in the audience, by virtue of the action alone, of these two "passions," or their presentation on the stage, directly in the characters acting, which then runs the risk of authorizing the first misunderstanding.[16]

3. The *pathemata* that undergo *katharsis* are not simply "passions" or "emotions": They are *painful* affects or troubles of the *pathē*, of *pathos* in general: that which is negative within *pathos*, the contrary of joy or pleasure. Whence the fallacious but invincible imperative of classicism, which Rousseau constantly opposes: the requirement to "please" ("touch" in the best case, according to Rousseau, and "flatter" in the worst).

4. The understanding of *katharsis* in its medical sense ("purgation," or even "homeopathic remedy" in the Hippocratic mode), which will wreak havoc up to at least Bernays and Freud, is probably derived from the famous passage of book VIII (1342), of the *Politics* on musical *katharsis*, where the medical usage of the term is explicitly metaphorical.[17] The blunder, which Nietzsche vigorously condemned (he had read Bernays and knew his classics), reaches its high point when the medical metaphor is, in turn, the object of a moral metaphorization, or when, under the term of discharge (*Entladung*), one confuses the two orders, or even three, if one also adds that of the psychopathological.[18]

But we suspect that Rousseau knows this, in his way. This is indeed why he searches for a way out, not without difficulty.

He believes he has found one in the interpretation, in fact a rather surprising one, that Crébillon offers in his preface to *Atrée* (1707). This interpretation has the merit of bringing the whole cathartic operation back to the simple arousal of pity—and of leading us back, by the same gesture, to the passage where we started, the one to which Rousseau was so attached that he wanted it inserted, after the fact, into the second *Discourse*:

> I hear it said that tragedy leads to pity through fear. So it does; but what is this pity? A fleeting and vain emotion which lasts no longer than the illusion which produced it; a vestige of natural sentiment soon stifled by the passions; a sterile pity which feeds on a few tears and which has never produced the slightest act of humanity. Thus, the sanguinary Sulla cried at the account of evils he had not himself committed. Thus, the tyrant of Phera hid himself at the theatre . . . [etc.] (LA 268)[19]

Between his admission of incomprehension and the recourse, obviously wholly "rhetorical," to this (false) solution, Rousseau never ceased accumulating arguments to show that theater, by its very nature, has no ethical or political efficacy. On the contrary.

We have already glimpsed the fact that previously, that is, practically from the start of his diatribe, he had denied theater any "power to change sentiments or morals, which it can only follow and embellish" (LA 264): "The sorts of Entertainment[20] are determined necessarily by the pleasure they give and not by their utility. If utility is there too, so much the better. But the principal object is to please; and, provided that the People enjoy themselves, this object is sufficiently attained" (LA 263). But this determination—the rule of classicism, therefore—suddenly became generalized: always and everywhere, theater is condemned to answer its viewers' expectations, to "flatter" them and to indulge their inclinations, to reflect their own image back to them. From this it follows that theater varies according to the "nations": The English want blood, the Italians want music, the French want gallantry, "love and civility" (LA 263); and according to history: Molière and Corneille are already no longer in season—a fortiori ancient tragedy: "Who doubts that the best Play of Sophocles would fall flat in our Theater?" (LA 264). In short, it follows "from these first observations that the general effect of the Theater is to strengthen the national character, to augment the natural inclinations, and to give a new energy to all the passions" (LA 265).

But the example of Sophocles, mentioned in passing, is revealing: a certain *identification*, of which, however, Rousseau had made so much in his theory of "natural pity" (if not of fear), is placed in doubt here. Regarding the question of the greatest play by Sophocles, Rousseau answered: "We would be unable to put ourselves in the places of men who are totally dissimilar to us" (LA 264). In other words, to condense things a bit, the attack aimed at the very mainspring of *katharsis* already indeed took the path of an initial challenge to any possible mimetic *mathēsis*—firmly rejected, as we know, in favor of reason alone. Rousseau had in reality understood quite well that it is *mimēsis* that authorizes *katharsis*. What he wanted to prove was that this "purgation" is not a purgation, or is of the order of mere *seeming* [*du semblant*], through the sole fact that it depends entirely on "semblance" in general, of this simulacrum-producing and "derealizing" activity that is *mimēsis*. Against all expectations, since, as we recall, only a "natural" mimetic faculty (one thus recognized as *mathematical*) could make it possible, in the second *Discourse*, to install the scene of origin. We have to believe that as soon as we "enter into theater," as Diderot puts it, as soon as culture and history have "suffocated" nature, *mimēsis* itself changes its nature: the "transport" that it supposes and that guaranteed, as its very *condition*, the recognition of likeness and the self, becomes the means par excellence of "illusion." Rousseau's entire demonstration is guided, in the *Letter*, by the presumed obviousness of this Platonic position. Meaning the "obviousness" of the power of contagion proper to *mimēsis*, or of the irrepressible or irremediable character of passionate *contamination*.

Everything is stated, or almost, beginning with the classicist invocation of the *Poetics*. "Is it possible that in order to become temperate and prudent we must begin by being intemperate and mad?" (LA 265). This was the first question, an incredulous one, brought to the surface by the enigma of purgation. And then Rousseau engages the debate:

"Oh no! It is not that," say the partisans of the Theater. "Tragedy certainly intends that all the passions which it portrays move us; but it does not always want our emotion to be the same as that of the character tormented by a passion. More often, on the contrary, its purpose is to excite sentiments in us opposed to those it lends its characters." They say, moreover, that if Authors abuse their power of moving hearts to excite an inappropriate interest, this fault ought to be attributed to the ignorance and depravity of the Artists and not to the art. They say, finally, that the faithful depiction of the passions and of the sufferings which accompany them suffices in itself to make us avoid them with all the care of which we are capable. (LA 265)

It makes little difference here whether we know exactly who these "partisans of theater" are (Du Bos, Porée, or perhaps even Diderot) and to what extent their argumentation is well founded. What is significant is obviously Rousseau's response, or rather his *reaction*. It is the voice of nature speaking, the pure interior feeling, the absolutely anterior "self" of innocence:

To become aware of the bad faith of all these responses, one need only consult one's own heart at the end of a tragedy. Do the emotion, the disturbance, and the softening which are felt within oneself and which continue after the play give indication of an immediate disposition to master and regulate our passions? Are the lively and touching impressions to which we become accustomed and which return so often, quite the means to moderate our sentiments in the case of need? Why should the image of the sufferings born of the passions efface that of the transports of pleasure and joy which are also seen to be born of them and which the Authors are careful to adorn even more in order to render their plays more enjoyable? (LA 265)

These few lines, as though written under the effect of a stupefaction, describe nothing other than the absolutely delicious moment of the "fall," the very vertigo of enjoyment in representation: this sort of ecstatic "engulfing" that Nietzsche will speak of in recalling the end of *Tristan*, and whose privilege Rousseau, without a doubt *despite himself*, will fiercely refuse to grant to art, so as to allow himself to feel it exclusively in the presence of nature: the Lac de Bienne of the "Fifth Walk," for example. (Hence Nietzsche's mockery and sarcasm against the "idyll," the reverie of the "noble savage" and the "culture of . . . opera"!) But this strange "alchemy" through which the "pains that are born of passions" are transmuted— or *transported*, if I can put it thus—into pleasure, is the cathartic effect itself. And Rousseau, this time, certainly *knows* this. The fact that he *denies* it—but in the (psychoanalytic) sense of *Verneinung* ("I do not want to know it"), not the fetishist *Verleugnung* ("I know it, but all the same")—is what constitutes the very mainspring of his prodigious creative capacity and the lacerated heart, the fundamental contradiction, of his work and thought. It is *right here* that we find this.

The rest of the demonstration is then no more than consequence (but Rousseau neglects no possible argument). In saying that it is *mimēsis* itself that is pernicious, and all the more so because it is *efficacious*, we have said everything. The reasons for this efficacy are, fundamentally, secondary. In order to gain the appropriate certainty, all that is required is to have experienced it. There is indeed, in the theater, a *purification* (*épuration*) of the affects or passions; but the danger lies precisely there:

> If, according to the observation of Diogenes Laertius, the heart is more readily touched by feigned ills than real ones, if theatrical imitations draw forth more tears than would the presence of the objects imitated, it is less because the emotions are feebler and do not reach the level of pain, as the Abbé du Bos believes, than because they are pure and without mixture of anxiety for ourselves. In giving our tears to these fictions, we have satisfied all the rights of humanity without having to give anything more of ourselves. (LA 268–269)

And a few lines later (where we will salute, in passing, the emergence of the "beautiful soul," hence forth destined to a prosperous future):

> In the final accounting, when a man has gone to admire fine actions in stories and to cry for imaginary miseries, what more can be asked of him? Is he not satisfied with himself? Does he not applaud his fine soul [*sa belle âme*]? Has he not acquitted himself of all that he owes to virtue by the homage which he has just rendered it? What more could one want of him? That he practice it himself? He has no role to play; he is no Actor. (LA 269)

The representation very nearly makes the world pass for a theater (or spectacle). This would be the saddest and most serious of "comic illusions."[21] The height of evil itself, which lies only in the deceptive lure of *purity*. In the moral sense, naturally . . .

We must note, nevertheless, that theater, or in any case tragedy, does not only derealize, in the sense I just evoked; nor does it only "exempt," to use Rousseau's term, who means by this that the identification with some character suffering on stage dispenses us from our *real* duties. But the theater, Rousseau says again, also "distances," under the effect of a double constraint, linked simultaneously to its historicity and to its formalism (its codification):

> The more I think about it, the more I find that everything that is played in the theater is not brought nearer

to us but made more distant. When I see the *Comte d'Essex*, the reign of Elizabeth is ten centuries removed in my eyes, and, if an event that took place yesterday at Paris were played, I should be made to suppose it in the time of Molière. The theater has rules, principles, and a morality apart, just as it has a language and a style of dress that is its own. We say to ourselves that none of this is suitable for us, and that we should think ourselves as ridiculous to adopt the virtues of its Heroes as it would be to speak in verse or to put on Roman clothing. (LA 269)

Now, this strangeness or distance, because it is in reality the very opposite of Brecht's *Verfremdungseffekt* (the "distantiation" which, for its part, is active and deliberate) with which it has been a bit too hastily confused, far from dissipating the practical or moral effect of identification (exemption), paradoxically reinforces it. The verdict is terrible:

This is pretty nearly the use of all these great sentiments and of all these brilliant maxims that are vaunted with so much emphasis—to relate them forever to the Stage [*la Scène*], and to present virtue to us as a theatrical game, good for amusing the public but which it would be folly seriously to attempt introducing into Society. Thus the most advantageous impression of the best tragedies is to reduce all the duties of man to some passing and sterile emotions that have no consequences, to make us applaud our courage in praising that of others, our humanity in pitying the ills that we could have cured, our charity in saying to the poor, God will help you! (LA 269)

It would doubtless be appropriate to take qualitative differences into consideration: we emerge, moved to tears, from a representation of *Bérénice* ("the emotion, turmoil, and tenderness"—it was *Bérénice* that Rousseau had in mind, as he admits later: *invitus invitam dimisit . . .*): *Le Comte d'Essex* (The Earl of Essex) is an instance of pompous and emphatic out-datedness, like tragedies "in the antique style." *Mimēsis* is efficacious only to the extent that it passes unnoticed and does not become ridiculous or stereotyped. But the ethical "delegation" remains the same. A contradiction may inhabit the stage (in general) and even haunt its effects: *mimēsis* of passion is not always contagious. The fact is that the practical effect, in general, is always equal to itself; and if there is "relief," in the absence of a "purging of passions," it is in virtue of the lessening of our obligations with respect to other people or ourselves. It is quite simply our *conscience* that is (illusorily) calmed. This is moreover why Rousseau can "supply" (or "supplement"), as he would have said, what is missing from Aristotle's *Poetics*: Comedy, which supposes a "simpler style" (LA 269) (a sort of realism, a drawing closer to us), fills a roughly analogous function in ridiculing virtue (see, once again, *The Misanthrope*); and we know that "ridicule . . . is the favorite arm of vice" (270). Identification, in comedy, is accompanied in a certain way by a projection, at the very least for Rousseau himself (or anyone who resembles him): is it not during the writing of the *Letter* that the first quarrel with Diderot took place because Rousseau had taken personally the judgment pronounced in the *Natural Son*: "only the bad man lives alone"? But for the "public," it is enough to feel released from any duty. Laughing, in the theater, and this can only mean laughing at what passes for serious, produces the same result as tears or admiration: We delegate onto the stage what weighs on us and pains us. *Katharsis* is nothing but a base respite; representation *excuses us*.

At bottom, this is what theater comes down to, in all its effects: *katharsis*, perhaps, but illusory or harmful.

2

At the end of these pages, everything seems finalized. The verdict is not only terrible, it is also irrevocable. Even before Rousseau seeks to confirm it by examples or attempts to administer proofs of it by examining certain tragic *subjects* (plot and character combined), the sentence comes down, with Aristotle once again providing support:

> Thus everything compels us to abandon this vain idea that some wish to give us of the perfection of a form of Theater directed toward public utility. It is an error . . . to hope that the true relations of things will be faithfully presented in the theater. For, *in general* [my emphasis], the Poet can only alter these relations in order to accommodate them to the taste of the public. In the comic, he diminishes them and sets them beneath man; in the tragic, he extends them to

render them heroic and sets them above humanity. Thus they are never to his measure, and we always see Beings *other than our own kind* [*nos semblables*] [my emphasis] in the theater. I add that this difference is so true and so well recognized that Aristotle makes a rule of it in his poetics: *Comoedia enim deteriores, Tragoedia meliores quam nunc sont imitari conantur.* Here is a well-conceived imitation, which proposes for its object that which does not exist at all and leaves, between defect and excess, that which is as a useless thing! But of what importance is the truth of the imitation, provided the illusion is there? The only object is to excite the curiosity of the public. These productions of wit and craft, like most others, have for their end only applause. When the Author receives it and the Actors share in it, the play has reached its goal, and no other advantage is sought. Now, if the benefit is nonexistent, the harm remains; and since the latter is indisputable, the issue seems to me to be settled. (LA 270)[1]

But if we look a bit closer here, things are not so simple. And especially not so simple as they are ordinarily thought to be.

Rousseau, in fact, *does not* condemn imitation *as such*. He condemns only "poetic," or "poietic" imitation: meaning any "production," whether it be "of the mind" or not, having no other aim than to *please*, in the most dubious sense of the term. If we were presented, at the theater, with "that which is," "Beings," *like* (or *as*)[2] "our fellows [*nos semblables*]," then the imitation would be "well-conceived [*bien entendüe*]" and we could then even speak of a "truth of imitation." But theater (re)presents nothing but illusion, for the simple reason that only illusion (or "fiction") is capable of "pleasing," no matter which means are used: laughter or tears. And this provides an immediate explanation of the fact that *katharsis* is in turn illusory: a relief that is deceptive or perverted, vain or harmful. "If the benefit [*le bien*] is nonexistent, the harm remains." But nothing forbids in principle the possibility of a good imitation, as well as an efficacious purging (if not purification) of the passions, as was the case, we remember, "at the origin."

It is consequently theater *itself* that Rousseau attacks. Or at least, theater as what it *became*: "a bit of theater [*du théâtre*]." We must consider the term "perfection" as decisive here; meaning, in its most elementary definition, the end of all "perfectibility": "Thus everything compels us to abandon this vain idea that some wish to give us of the perfection of a form of Theater." According to a schema that we already know, Rousseau does not in the least condemn art; but he nurtures the hope of a "perfected art," meaning an "art" (re)become "nature," sublating[3] the very opposition from which it was born. Through the mediation of Kant, as we know, this is a lesson that Schiller will retain, and he will even make it a point to explicate and extend it to its furthest consequences: it will be the entire object of his reflection on the "naïve" and "sentimental" in literature; but also on the possibility offered to "modern" theater to sublate the opposition between ancient tragedy and tragedy of the "classical" period.[4]

"Perfected art," Jean Starobinski notes, is an expression that figures in the first version (known as the Geneva manuscript) of the *Social Contract*: "It is necessary 'to draw from the ill itself the remedy that should cure it,' for, if man knows it and wants it, he will find again 'in perfected art the reparation of the ills that the beginnings of art caused to nature.'"[5] And Starobinski, who notices this schema regarding musical imitation in the *Essay on the Origin of Languages*, adds that "the same idea, formulated in other terms, reappears at the beginning of *Emile*."[6]

But "drawing the remedy from the illness" is the goal of the cathartic operation itself, at least in its medical interpretation (to which Rousseau subscribes as if it went without saying). And we perhaps begin to suspect that the speculative *Aufhebung*, indeed, will not be greatly distanced from this interpretation of *katharsis*, if not explicitly conceived on its model. I will return to this in a moment.

The fact remains that a certain origin of the theater allows us to glimpse a theater different from "a bit of theater [*du théâtre*]," and consequently to expect something else—not, doubtless, from "the Stage in general," but in any case from "Plays [*Spectacles*]." Thinking a truth of imitation and an efficacy of purgation is not out of the question. There remains the task of grasping the "truth of the theater" (the expression is Rousseau's), and its "utility," in its very essence, or in its origin, in its state of "perfection,"[7] which is to say, in its Greek moment, which forms an absolute *exception*. Before the "Stage."

Rousseau comes back to the point twice.

The first time occurs when, at the end of the review of examples, all taken from modern French theater and serving to illustrate his first major conclusion (the one that we have just read), Rousseau attempts to define what in his view a good tragic character might be, or the "character" that a good imitation might present. He analyzes Crébillon's *Catilina* and Voltaire's *Rome sauvée*, which is a response to it; *Mahomet*, also by Voltaire; and finally *Atrée et Thyeste* by Crébillon. The result of the analysis is given in advance: "the French Stage, undeniably the most perfect, or at least, the most correct which has ever existed, is no less the triumph of the great villains than of the most illustrious heroes: witness Catalina, Mahomet, Atreus and many others" (LA 271). Between the "villains [*scelerats*]" especially the "black Atreus," and the overly sublime "Heroes" lies nothing: no one, no *man*, not one of our "fellows." Only Thyestes is an exception; but, however surprising this may seem, it is because he corresponds point by point with what one imagines as the ideal of the "tragic character" according to Aristotle, meaning Oedipus, and Thyestes.[8] Rousseau speaks, not of Seneca, but of Crébillon's "remake":

Before finishing with this play, I cannot refrain from mentioning a merit in it which will, perhaps, seem to be a fault to many people. The role of Thyestes is, perhaps of all that have ever been put on our stage, the one that most approaches the taste of the ancients. He is not a courageous Hero; he is not a model of virtue; it could not be said, either, that he is a criminal [*scelerat*]. He is a weak man and nevertheless involves our sympathy on this basis alone: he is a man and unfortunate. It seems, also, on this basis alone, that the feeling which he inspires is extremely tender and moving. For this man is very close to each of us; heroism, on the other hand, overwhelms us even more than it moves us, because, after all, what has it to do with us? Would it not be desirable if our sublime Authors deigned to descend a little from their customary great heights and touched us sometimes with simple suffering humanity, for fear that having pity for only unhappy Heroes we shall pity no one? (LA 273–274)[9]

And Rousseau adds immediately: "The ancients had Heroes and put men on their stages; we, on the contrary, put only Heroes on the stage and hardly have any men. The ancients spoke of humanity in less-studied phrases, but they knew how to exercise it better" (LA 274 [for all quotations in this paragraph]). The question is thus tacitly posed, and it is inevitable: why, after all, did the ancient stage (which the modern one imitates, indeed, most of the time) also display so many "monsters," and such terrible "monsters" as these? Oedipus, Phaedra, Medea, of course; but also Agamemnon, "sacrificing his daughter," and Orestes "cutting his mother's throat," and several others as well? Why these odious crimes and the "atrocious actions," which doubtless succeed in "making the plays interesting and in giving exercise to the virtues," but which at the same time "accustom the eyes of the people to horrors that they ought not even to know and to crimes they ought not to suppose possible"? How could the Greeks accept the lessons of such plays (which teach us only "that man is not free and that Heaven punishes him for crimes that it makes him commit" (*Oedipus*), and "how cruel and unnatural a mother can be made by the rage of jealousy" (*Medea*)), and how could they *tolerate* the view of an evil so radical that it seems unimaginable or impossible?

Rousseau's response must be read very attentively; we will soon find, with the help of a few additional remarks, its speculative translation in one of Schelling's very first texts:

If the Greeks *tolerated* such theater it was because it represented for them national traditions which were always common among the people, which they had reasons to recall constantly; *and even its hateful aspects were part of its intention*. Deprived of the same motives and the same concern [*intérest*], how can the same tragedy find, among your people [that is, among the French, the "gentlest and the most humane people on Earth"[10]] spectators *capable of enduring* the depictions it presents to them and the characters which are given life in it? (LA 275, my emphases)

In other words, and to speak with Nietzsche (who will ask the same question), what, then, was the Greeks' degree of *tolerance* of suffering and horror? Of the "hateful [or odious, *odieux*]," since this is the very moral word that Rousseau uses? Or, to translate back into Aristotle's language, how did the Greeks take pleasure in so much pain? Or so much unpleasure, if this time we use Freud's lexicon—that, for example, of "Psychopathic Characters on the Stage"?[11]

Rousseau's response, unlike many others that came after it, is not formulated in an Aristotelian mode (or at least a mode presumed to be such): it includes nothing that might authorize an *aesthetic* interpretation, in the sense of a psychophysiology (Bernays, Nietzsche) or a psychopathology (Freud). And if it remains obviously overdetermined by the moral ("classical") reading of Aristotle, the pressure that Plato exerts is nevertheless such that it is first of all, and essentially, *political*. Or historico-political. But, by the *same* token, and this is completely surprising, it runs *exactly* contrary to what Plato wanted to signify: the Greeks, if they didn't "believe" (really) "in their myths," were at least used to them, and had good (political) reasons to recall them, even if only "national" reasons. They believed in their own history (Heidegger will transcribe: in their historial *Dasein*[12]), this was even the core of their religion, simultaneously in the sense of *relegere* ("gathering") and *religare* ("binding"): tradition, or memory; and political bond, or state (polity). At roughly the period of the writing of the *Letter*, Rousseau has Saint-Preux write, from Paris (and this motif will reappear in a moment in the *Letter* itself): "The institution of tragedy had, for its inventors, a religious grounding . . . Greek tragedies hung upon real events or ones reputed to be real by the audience."[13] Which signifies unequivocally that not only was the imitation not fabricated, but that *katharsis* had a very real effect: the imitation in this case was not of a pretended "reality" (in the sense of a "realism" or a "verism"), nor is it, equally, that of some lost sublimity: it was an imitation—and this is the measure of its *accuracy* [*justesse*]—of what Hegel will call, precisely in reference to Aeschylus (*The Eumenides*) or to Sophocles (*Antigone*), *die Sittlichkeit*: let us call it "ethicity" or the "ethical world." The theater of the Greeks, because it was *mimēsis* (presentation) of the Greek *ethos*, was instructive; it was "useful." And the reason for this is very simple: *it was not "of theater [du théâtre]."*

This is confirmed much further on, with a surprising argumentative vigor and a sort of intoxication in its eloquence ("Dionysos!" said Hölderlin), in the second convocation of the Greek *example*, which also means the "Greek exception." It arrives in the course of a very long development on the actor, the mimetic man, and his morality. We already know that Rousseau repeats quite closely the Platonic demonstration. But he stumbles, all the same, against the "universal" condemnation which, beginning in Rome, is visited upon actors: *quisquis in scenam prodierit . . . infamis est.* And he stumbles all the more in that this condemnation (penal, moral, etc.: this decree of infamy) was transmitted by the Church all the way up to the present day, and because, probably, it was "only the result of prejudice." But no objection can stand: "I could impute these prejudices to the declamations of the Priests, if I did not find them established among the Romans before the birth of Christianity and not only vaguely current in the spirit of the People but authorized by express laws which declared the actors disreputable, stripped them of the name and rights of Roman Citizens, and put the actresses in the class of prostitutes" (LA 307). Rousseau then refutes a number of misleading arguments, at which point, suddenly, it is the Greeks who "enter the scene." The "spectacle" is fabulous indeed:

I know of only one people which did not have the same maxims as all the others about this; that is the Greeks. It is certain that among them the profession of the Theater was so little indecent that Greece furnishes examples of Actors charged with certain public functions either in the State or on Embassies. But the reasons for this exception can easily be found. (I) Since Tragedy, as well as Comedy, was invented by the

Greeks, they could not in advance put a mark of contempt on an estate the effects of which they did not yet know, and, when they began to be known, public opinion was already fixed. (2) Since Tragedy had something sacred in its origin, at first its actors were regarded as Priests rather than Buffoons. (3) Since all the subjects of the Plays were drawn exclusively from the national antiquities which the Greeks idolized, they saw in these actors less men who played fables than educated Citizens who performed the history of their country so that it could be seen by their compatriots. (4) This People, so enthusiastic about its liberty as to believe that the Greeks were the only men free by nature, recalled with a vivid sentiment of pleasure its ancient misfortunes and the crimes of its Masters. These great depictions ceaselessly instructed this people who could not prevent themselves from feeling some respect for the organs of this instruction. (5) Tragedy was at first played only by men, so that in their theater this scandalous mixture of men and women, which makes of our theaters so many schools of bad morals, was not to be seen. (6) Finally, their performances had none of the meanness of today's; their theaters were not built by interest and avarice, they were not closed up in dark prisons; their actors had no need to make collections from the spectators or to count out of the corner of their eye the number of people whom they saw coming in the door to be sure of their supper.

These great and proud entertainments [*spectacles*], given under the Sky before a whole nation, presented on all sides only combats, victories, prizes, objects capable of inspiring the Greeks with an ardent emulation and of warming their hearts with sentiments of honor and glory. It is in the midst of this imposing array, so fit to elevate one and stir the soul, that the actors, animated with the same zeal, shared, according to their talents, the honors rendered to the conquerors of the games, often the first men of the nation. I am not surprised that, far from abasing them, their profession, exercised in this manner, gave them that pride of courage and that noble disinterestedness which seemed sometimes to raise the actor to the level of his role. With all of this, never was Greece, Sparta excepted, cited as an example of good morals; and Sparta, which tolerated no theater, was not concerned with honoring those who appeared in it. (LA 308–309)

There is no doubt that Rousseau is mistaken: there was indeed a theater in Sparta, as was pointed out to him later; and in fact he conceded the point.[14] But what matters to him, in mentioning Sparta and thus holding it in opposition to Athens, is saving a Greece pure of any accusation of immorality. The mention of Sparta, at the end of this literally *sublime* page, is meant simply to emphasize that, *even* in Athens, theater was not "of theater"; and thereby also to mark out the terrain— the precaution is certainly not useless—of the final

"Civic Festival," for which the model will be openly Lacedaemonian.[15]

It is no accident if I use the word *sublime*; and I use it not only because we are dealing here with questions of *elevation* (*heben, erheben, erhaben*, etc.), which would already be sufficient. But also because, in the series of arguments put forth, in the conclusive mention of "these great and *proud* [*superbe*] [one must indeed emphasize this] spectacles given under Heaven, before an entire nation"; the essential is this (this is the fourth argument): "This people, so enthusiastic about its liberty as to believe that the Greeks were the only men free by nature, recalled with a vivid sentiment of pleasure its ancient misfortunes and the crimes of its Masters." A pure paradox: this people, drunk on its freedom, admittedly the first—and perhaps only—people-subject in History, *autonomous* and conscious of itself as such, but also *possessed* by freedom, falling prey to a sort of furor or *mania* of freedom (Plato's term for the madness of the Greeks: Hölderlin and Nietzsche will seek, on the path here reopened, to penetrate its mystery), experienced the most intense pleasures—joy or *jouissance*—in *presentation* and *remembrance*, meaning at the *thought* (*mens, memoria; denken, andenken*, etc.), of the horror of its time of servitude. The spectacle of this horror was not only *delicious*, in the most literal sense (which Burke will retain); it also gave rise to *thought*, as Kant will say regarding the sublime—here, the very Idea of freedom—; it *instructed*, in the sense in which, for example, one could speak of an "aesthetic education of man": its power of *liberation* and *elevation* (which are the same) was rigorously *mathematical*. To put it another way, tragedy *purified* down to its essence the fanatical—the fatal or "destinal"— freedom that was born, among the Greeks, from its very *negation*: from *tyranny*, as the entire rest of the century will repeat after Rousseau, until the reversal (*Umkehrung*, as Hölderlin says) that will sanction its end. Until the *Revolution*. Or, if you will—but I will discuss this again later—until the "peripeteia." Hölderlin, because he had read Rousseau, will translate the title of Sophocles's play as *Oedipus the Tyrant*; and will turn *Antigone* into a "republican" play.[16]

Katharsis is in the form of *Aufhebung* (purification in the form of sublation): *aufheben*, in any case, will "translate" *kathairein*—I will provide proof of this very shortly. But this *translation*, in which the entire future of philosophy will be in play, will not only be possible through Rousseau's establishment (without formalizing it as such) of dialectical logic itself as the logic of the relationship between "nature" and its other(s). (He himself, like Diderot somewhat later, spoke only of "paradox" and based his most exigent discourse on the figure of the oxymoron.) It also made it necessary for Rousseau to establish it on the example of Attic tragedy, and to turn Greece into a *historical exception*.

This is what explains why the purification at stake here would be first of all *the purification of Greece itself* (this proud little people, scornful and warlike, as Nietzsche will say more or less). A purification that is fur-thermore much more audacious—but did Rousseau know this?—than the one that the Germans will too blithely credit to his contemporary Winckelmann, if only because this one is a *true* purification, not shrink-ing from horror or insanity, but looking at it directly, not being terrified by it, maintaining it, etc. The purification of Greece consists in the negation of its negativity. It con-denses itself and comes to light in the formula: *The Greek theater was not "of the theater [du théâtre]*," this formula that Heidegger will repeat in somnambular fashion until the 1930s, imagining that it came from Hegel.[17] But this properly *apophatic* formula may hence-forth be used for almost anything: at least for almost everything that falls, if we dare say it here, under Art or Culture, *tekhnē* in general, that which appears at first sight to be "added" (it is the "supplement"), not truly pres-ent, fabricated, reproduced, delegated, etc. It is, at bottom, the *Socratic facility.* And in fact, Rousseau did indeed read Plato. But at the very moment when he brings him back (let us not forget that this "rehabilitation" of Greece takes its place within a long—and Platonic—development on *hypocrisy* itself, on the fallacious, harmful and con-tagious "art" of the actor[18]), he *overturns* it properly speaking, thus inaugurating what we might call the philosophical theater of the future, in which the nega-tion of Platonism will not cease to be its verification.

Everything happens, in fact, as if Rousseau *knew* that Plato wrote *The Republic* the very year (in 385) when tragedy ceased to exist, in any case as it had existed before: contest (*agōn*), unique representation, cult of Dionysos, virtually compulsory festival or ceremony; and where there had begun to take root, all over Greece (outside of Attica alone), a "repertory theater," dedicated to replaying the "classics," from Aeschylus to Euripides—this *theater* (*ta theatra*) on which precisely, fifty years later, the teachings of Aristotle will focus. In sum, something "belated."

However—and this is Rousseau's astonishing intuition—there is *another Greece*, pre-Platonic, or, as some will be quick to say, "pre-Socratic." A Greece *absolutely anterior*, and consequently *purely archaic*. And harboring, in its native, *original perfection*, its own negation: Hellenistic decadence, Romanization; finally, Christianity—which is its false sublation or, and it amounts to the same, its retransmission *in negative form*. And certainly its aggravation.[19] It is a matter, quite simply, of a new *exemplum*: Rousseau "invents" (which is to say, discovers) what we today call "another scene." But which is precisely not yet, and will no longer be in the future, a *scene* (a stage), though it does bring this possibility—this danger.[20]

At bottom, this page where we read the first (Platonic) overturning of Platonism installs, and durably so, the modern *myth* of Greece: indeed, an entire *philosophical scene*. Doubtless, there are in this anterior Greece—or, what amounts to the same, in this pretheatrical tragedy—quite a few elements missing, which only the German philologists will make it their task to contribute: the cho-rus, the two spaces (the *orkhestra* and the *skēnē*), the music, the two languages, the Dionysian cult, the matri-cial oxymoron of the dramas or of their proper names (Oedipus: he who, having seen, knows; Antigone: born against, or the woman against, to give only the major ex-amples), enthusiasm and sobriety, drunkenness and dream, unpresentable horror and figuration, the Erinyes and Athena, Apollo and Juno (or Dionysus and Apollo), the two laws (of night and day, of blood and *logos*), sex-ual difference, etc. Doubtless also, Rousseau's Greece is too "political," meaning too republican or democratic (and, finally, too Spartan): actors who are nothing but educated citizens or statesmen, which one does not per-ceive as performers, but rather as the officiants of a "civil religion," the so-to-speak mnemotechnic repetitions of the opposition between mastery and servitude, the glo-rification of "national antiquities," the "theater" as civic education, the free access to state art . . . all of this will perhaps still please Schiller somewhat but, with Napo-leon past (and Rome reinstalled), practically none of his successors, with the exception of Marx. This does not change the fact that Rousseau is indeed the first—insisting as he does on his desire to understand the tragic *effect*, meaning the cathartic operation—to con-ceive of the "anterior" Greece (tragedy) as the site of a fundamental *antagonism*: the very one that is simulta-neously hidden and revealed by the contradiction, or the paradox, of the tragic effect as *sublimation*: the joy inspired by the (re)presentation of horror, which is none other than the paradox of the free joy experienced at the (re)presentation of unpresentable Freedom.[21] That is (to translate), the pleasure taken in the denunciation of an immemorial servitude. It is moreover no coincidence that, indicating this antagonism, Rousseau insists to such a degree on the *agonistic* culture of the Greeks, happily common to Athens and Sparta, "theater" and Games, sacred ceremony and festive communion: "These great and proud entertainments . . . presented on all sides only combats, victories, prizes, objects capable of inspiring the Greeks with an ardent emulation and of warming their hearts with sentiments of honor and glory. It is in the midst of this imposing array, so fit to elevate one and stir the soul," etc. (LA 308). And it is therefore also no coincidence that the civic Festival, so apt to give birth to "pure joy" which consists only in "public joy,"[22] and which is itself—once again in a pure oxymoron—a *popular-aristocratic* festival where, each person within his own profession and proper place ("one man, one job," as Leo Strauss said), strives, by virtue of healthy emulation, to become "King"—"of the harquebus, the cannon, and navigation"—and to excel *in (and as) what he is*, for the greatest pleasure, and the sovereign good of the community.

We know all too well, no doubt (if only for having laughed at it so much), this very famous "number"—half-realist (descriptive), half-utopian (fictive, "projective")—in which Rousseau declares his wishes for the Republican

Festival. I resolve all the same to quote it, at least in order to emphasize, as we proceed, the persistence of the Platonic (or simply Greek) lexicon and the strict conceptual apparatus, and the power of cohesion, that govern it. Politically, we know—or think we know—the consequences, meaning the "applications," of which this text was the cause or the occasion; philosophically, I am not sure the same is true, and certain effects are perhaps, as always, incalculable.[23] (If I make a few deletions here and there, it is, as Rousseau would say, as a simple means of *economy*, for which I may well be forgiven.)

What! Ought there to be no Entertainments [*Spectacle*] in a Republic? On the contrary, there ought to be many. It is *in Republics* that they were *born*, it is in their bosom that they are seen to flourish with a truly *festive* air. To what peoples is it more fitting to *assemble* often and form among themselves sweet *bonds* of *pleasure* and *joy* than to those who have so many reasons to *like one another* and remain forever *united*? We already have many of these public festivals; let us have even more; I will be only the more charmed for it. But let us not adopt these *exclusive* Entertainments which *close up a small number of people* in melancholy fashion in a *gloomy cavern*, which keep them *fearful* and immobile in silence and *inaction*, which gives them only prisons, lances, soldiers, and *afflicting images of servitude and inequality* to see. No, happy Peoples, these are not your festivals. It is *in the open air, under the sky* that you ought to *gather* and give yourselves to the sweet sentiment of your happiness. Let your pleasures not be *effeminate* or *mercenary*; let nothing that has an odor of *constraint* and *selfishness poison* them; let them be *free* and *generous* like you are, let the *sun* illuminate your *innocent* entertainments; *you will constitute one yourselves*, the *worthiest* it can illuminate.

But what then will be the objects of these entertainments? What will be shown in them? *Nothing*, if you will. With liberty, wherever abundance reigns, *well-being* also reigns. Plant a stake crowned with flowers in the middle of a square; *gather the people together there*, and you will have a festival. Do better yet; *let the Spectators become an Entertainment to themselves* [*donnez les Spectateurs en Spectacle*]; *make them actors themselves; do it so that each sees and loves himself in the others so that all will be better united.* I need not have recourse to the *games of the ancient Greeks*; there are *modern* ones which are still in existence, and I find them precisely in our city. Every year we have reviews, public prizes, *Kings* of the harquebus, the cannon, and sailing. Institutions so *useful* and so *agreeable* cannot be too much multiplied; *of such Kings there cannot be too many.* Why should we not do to make ourselves active and robust what we do to become skilled in the use of arms? Has the Republic less need of workers than of soldiers? Why should we not found, on the model of the military prizes, other prizes for *Gymnastics*, *wrestling* [*la lutte*], running, discus, and the various bodily exercises? Why should we not animate our Boatmen by *contests* [*joûtes*] on the Lake? ... All festivals of this sort are expensive only insofar as one wishes them to be, and the *gathering* [*concours*] alone renders them quite magnificent. Nevertheless, one must have been there with the Genevans to understand with what ardor they devote themselves to them. *They are unrecognizable*; they are no longer that steady people which never deviates from its *economic rules*. ... The people are lively, gay, and tender; their hearts are then in their eyes as they are always on their lips; they seek to *communicate their joy* and *their pleasures*. ... *All the societies constitute but one, all become common to all*. ... It would be the image of Lacedaemon if a certain *lavishness* [*profusion*] did not prevail here; but this very lavishness is at this time *in its place*, and the sight of abundance makes that of the *liberty* which produces it *more moving*.[24] (LA 343–345)

It would of course be necessary to provide an "economic" commentary on this page (or a socioeconomic one, which is less liable to confusion). Just as it would have been necessary to include in our considerations, in the presentation of this Festival—and, following it, of its nocturnal episode, the dance—the very long developments that Rousseau devotes to the "question of women" and the social division of the sexes.[25] This is hardly possible here, where I would like to remain focused, at least if such a dividing line can be traced out, on the sole question of theater. Or rather, henceforth, the question of its sublation, its *Aufhebung*. We can see without difficulty: the sky, the open air, the sunshine, the glorification (not to say: the "cult") of freedom, the generalized *agōn* (contest and competition, emulation, triumph of the best), etc., all of this is Greek tragedy, but Greek tragedy *without the stage*, without the *scene*, that is, without *the* germinal divisions of what will become "theater"—or "opera": stage-orchestra, spectacle-spectators. I do indeed use the word "stage [*scène*]" in the modern (Italian) sense of the term, both in order to simplify, or facilitate, and in order not to say "representation"; for there is indeed, in the Festival or the Spectacle (Rousseau does not maintain the word out of carelessness or for lack of a better one), *representation*, even if in the form of *auto-representation*: representation of *nothing*, says Rousseau, if not of the spectators themselves.

Mimēsis of *nothing* (or of *no one*, if not of the best of the *self*, and in the *self*), is *play [le jeu]*. (Schiller, again, at the end of the *Letters on the Aesthetic Education of Man*: Man is not truly man except when he plays, etc.) This is moreover the reason why the "monument" of the Greeks is not Athens but Sparta—had there been a theater in Sparta; and had this theater been (re)constructed from stone by the Romans. . . . The apparatus [*dispositif*] of the game, or of the Games, is *almost* nil; I am not saying: an apparatus without apparatus. It takes only a *sign* indicating that the Festival will take place (the stake planted in a square, around which the people gather) or that the contest is open: in the naval joust that Rousseau imagines on the lake, a passage which I did not quote (but everyone remembers this), the "Flag planted at the finish" (LA 344). It is not stated, at least not explicitly, who organizes these festivals: doubtless the Council, the city magistrates, but they are not mentioned anywhere. The Festival, to be "civic" (political), must be *almost* spontaneous. There must at least be an agreement to plan the occasion. Or a custom, as in the "scene," which precisely is not one, or only *barely*, of the regiment of Saint-Gervais. For the Festival, as Hölderlin will say, can only be a "Festival of peace," *Friedensfeier*. (Where did Heidegger, who made so much of this poem, think that Hölderlin could have taken this motif?) The *agōn* is not at all a "fight [*lutte*] to the death," as it was perhaps for the Greeks, in the "Greek moment," if we adopt Hegel's terminology. This is why it inspires only the "joy" of being-together or reunion, which is the truth of the "pleasure" that the theater, since "Aristotle," had illusorily given itself the obligation (the rule) to satisfy. And if such a "joy" must necessarily include *effusion*, this effusion is not, for all that, *fusion*, it does not at all forbid each person from being him- or herself. The Festival, on the contrary, is a festival of appropriation. In Rousseau there is something *sentimental*, in Schiller's sense of this term, since this is the "poietic" and "praxic" regime of the (modern) subject.[26] But nothing "fusional." Nor anything, moreover, that could suggest any kind of *putting into practice*: this festival that greatly glorifies properly *technical* skill does not make a claim—which is to say, precisely *no longer* makes a claim—to "art," but boasts, on the contrary, what Kant will call "art re-become nature." Meaning *barely* art, or "facile" arts: a decorated post (later, a "tree of liberty"? Hölderlin, Schelling, and Hegel will believe this one day), an embroidered flag, a little military music to which one can dance ... Sparta with Plato, no doubt. But Nature, too: the lake, for example, with—dare I say it—the mountains as "backdrop." And everywhere a circulation of freedom, the joy of pure relationships, the feeling of "sweet bonds." For the community, if one neither establishes it, nor installs it as a work of art, is in reality the very *articulation* of the agents, or of the happy *actors* who compose and enjoy it. This is the meaning of the calmed, relieved *agōn*, withdrawn from pain (and, first of all, from work, suffering, and all violence), in short *purified*. Or *cured*. This cure—*katharsis* itself—is *naivety* (which never was, and especially not at the origin) finally realized, accomplished: man, in his "promise" (in Malherbe's sense), complete. Or *almost*.

This "almost," or "hardly," which necessarily modalizes *all* the concepts that Rousseau uses here or that we, in reading him, are obliged to use, means evidently that the "Spectacle" is still a spectacle, that the absence of stage is still a "Stage," that spontaneity is not without a code, that "Art" is indeed art, and "naivety" indeed a naivety. I have tried to exclude, with respect to the disposition of the Festival, the rhetorical—and syntagmatic—facility of the "without [*sans*]" (which can nevertheless *be written*, as Jacques Derrida reminds us, as "blood [*sang*]"): apparatus *without* apparatus, for example. Because this "turn" hides, or allows us too comfortably to "turn," another *turn*, a true one, if I may say so: a *trope*, a *figure* ("of words"), in this case *oxymoron*, which is constantly determining and punctuating the description, if it is a description, of the Festival; and which is condensed in the response—"Nothing, if you will"—to the question: "But what *then* [*enfin*, my emphasis] will be the object of these spectacles? What will be shown in them?" or reappears in the formula: "let the Spectators become a Spectacle to themselves." Which is immediately translated as: "Make them actors themselves." (Which we, *in turn*, cannot help retranslating as: Make them actors *of* themselves. In which case— though unfortunately I cannot insist on the point—the Festival would be the time outside of time, a suspended, ecstatic time of enjoyment, of the *jouissance* of self: of seeing-oneself-doing and of pure existing, in internal difference or breakdown, in "extimacy," as Lacan says, in the most interior outside-of-oneself; in the same way, at bottom, as in *jouissance* "itself," perhaps the hearing-oneself-sing (of the *Essay*), or in any case the unexperienced experience of death commemorated in absolutely paradoxical fashion in the "Second Walk" of the *Reveries*.[27] I would add, for my part: the fact of being, but Rousseau would have perhaps admitted this. If at least he had been able to agree not to reduce this problem of intimate theatricality, or of intimate *dramatization*, to the Augustinian question of, or obsession with, confession, precisely, the question of sincerity and "transparency.")

We must, nevertheless, know how to cut things short.

Two remarks are necessary here.

The first is to say that the figure that suddenly flashes out in the "Nothing"—grudgingly attenuated with an "if you will"—that Rousseau suddenly poses as the truth of the "Spectacle" (nothing will be shown in them; "*nothing*," the "thing itself," will (not) be offered as a spectacle), the *oxymoron*, then, before being the figure of contradiction, is one of the *impossible*. The Festival is the impossible itself, as will be the democracy of the *Contract*, which would require "a people of gods." At least. . . . As Hölderlin will say, while undergoing the "very severe" lesson of his readings: "the immediate, strictly speaking, is impossible for mortals, as for immortals./ . . . But strict mediacy is the Law."[28] Because the impossible is the necessity of ek-sistence or, if you prefer, the impossibility and impracticability of what in this case we could call the *in-stance*, or even *in-sistence*—in itself, and in relation to the other—it is also the ultrapolitical "law" of politics: a law from before any law, like that invoked by Antigone, higher (more sublime) than any law—which I will call here the law of *semblance* or of *simulation* in general, which is the law of the Same [*du Même*]: of Being-self or Being-same [*l'Être-même*], of the Thing-itself or the Thing-as-same [*la Chose-même*], of Being-itself or Being-a-self [*l'Être-soi-même*], and, consequently, of any *relation* of any kind (starting with the "relation to the other").[29] It is the *archi-nomos* of *mimēsis* "itself." A sort of transcendental simulation. Nothing is present without being in some manner (re)presented: in (re)presentation. Hence, in order to speak of the impossible Festival, meaning the impossible ending of (re)presentation, one is obliged to turn to the figure of the oxymoron: the impossible is pure contradiction. Hence, too, the initial, original oxymoron, the *zōon politikon phusei*, which was to be broken or excluded, ends up at the "end," if it is an end, in what is proposed, in any case, as the final stage of the deconstruction of the "establishment" or the apparatus of representation, of theatrical *installation*. And of political installation, it amounts to the same. But *concealed*, obligatorily; more or less concealed; and all the same, perfectly visible: a people of princes, a workers' (laborers') aristocracy, a pacified *agōn*, an emulation without rivalry, a space of play which is not a stage, a "useful" festival, etc. The deconstruction, in reality, just barely hides all that it leaves intact, meaning the essential. And even, *last but not least*,[30] money, very hypocritically placed in security (there are prizes for the contests, if only a flag; Genevan "lavishness" and "abundance," which are not enough for state subsidies, or for maintaining a theater, make the aspect of the "liberty" that "produces them" "more touching"). Or war, *in extremis* evoked in a word (but all the same, exemplary Greece or not, without slavery):

> Thus did that Sparta, which I shall have never cited enough as the example that we ought to follow, recall its citizens by modest festivals and games without pomp; thus in Athens, in the midst of the fine arts, thus in Susa, in the lap of luxury and softness, the bored Spartan longed for his coarse feasts and his fatiguing exercises. It is at Sparta that, in laborious idleness, everything was pleasure and entertainment; it is there that the harshest labors passed for recreation and that small relaxations formed a public instruction; it is there that the citizens, constantly assembled, consecrated the whole of life to amusements which were the great business of the state and to games from which they relaxed only for war. (LA 349)

My second remark will be a bit briefer: it concerns, as one might have suspected for a certain time now, *Aufhebung*, sublation; and the logic, even the origin of the logic here in operation, or set to work. I have sometimes been able to say that the Festival sublates tragedy; sometimes, more strangely, that it purifies it. As though *Aufhebung* translated *katharsis*. That is indeed what I meant. With just one reservation, which is not a mere precaution: not only did Rousseau never think in German, or, still less, with the linguistico-speculative virtuosity of Hegel;[31] not only would he have needed to read

Kant, who would have to have already read him, before leaving the "Tenth Walk" in suspense—recalling for the last time, one "Palm Sunday," the "most loving of all women"; he would also have had to know that *katharsis* is unquestionably not able to signify "cleansing" (hardly "relief," and certainly not a "calming effect [*apaisement*]"[32]).

Well, he didn't know this.

This does not in the least prevent—and his first major readers will even see Knowledge as such in this, or Science—the logic underlying *all* his texts where *theatricality* is in question, and thus his reading of Aristotle, from being truly a *dialectical* logic, in the post-Kantian sense of the term, according to which every "negative" is "picked up [*ramassé*]," as one translates into Alsatian the so closely neighboring Swabian, removed [*dérobé*], taken away [*enlevé*] and raised up [*élevé*], sheltered, conserved, always there, discernible and to be discerned, symptomatic, indelible, kept and *guarded*, to say it all (*bewahren, wahr, Wahrheit*, etc.: *truth* itself, regard and respect [*l'égard*]). Insofar as one does not deny theatricality, precisely: (re)presentation, *mimēsis*, semblance and simulation. Which Rousseau, it is obvious, could not fail to do, even while knowing very well, as his *nearly* incomparable rhetoric clearly shows, that he was doing it. Out of *duty*, without a doubt, since in fact history assigned the obligation. As always.

3

In the well-known opening lines of his *Essay on the Tragic*, Peter Szondi says, in substance: since Aristotle, there has been a poetics of tragedy; since Schelling, there is a philosophy of the tragic.[1] This proposition is only half correct. There is indeed no doubt a "philosophy of the tragic," which is illustrated by Schelling, Hegel and Hölderlin, as well as Kierkegaard and Nietzsche, Freud (and Lacan), Rosenzweig and Benjamin, Bataille, Heidegger—and a few others. But this philosophy of the tragic is still, and always, a poetics of tragedy. This could be verified in *every* case, without exception. There is not a single philosophy of the tragic which is not, admittedly or not, a commentary on Aristotle, meaning that its starting point, explicitly or not, is the question—or the enigma—of the *tragic effect*.

I would like, in order to finish, to take just one example. The first one given (it is the one with which Szondi began his demonstration), but equally because it is indeed inaugural and, as such, one of the most discussed. It is the *example* itself: we see in it how, around the *figure* of Oedipus and the "libretto," Nietzsche would have said, of Sophocles's *Oedipus Rex*, there develops, in matrix state, and in keeping with a Kantian reading of Rousseau (a sort of palimpsest where, between the lines of the "transcendental dialectic" of the first *Critique*, we might decipher entire sentences from the *Letter to d'Alembert*), the very onto-logic of German idealism, meaning the *speculative dialectic*. Which supposes, de facto as well as de jure, a *theater*: *mimēsis* itself, and its *cathartic* power.

This example, one may have recognized, is the tenth and last of the *Philosophical Letters on Dogmatism and Criticism*, written in 1795 (Schelling was barely twenty years old[2]), where the work of art in general—and tragedy in particular—to the extent that they are par excellence (re)presentation, *mimēsis* or *Darstellung*, offer the possibility of a resolution of the fundamental contradiction of Reason, in the Kantian sense: meaning in this case the irreducible opposition between the recognition of Necessity (Spinoza's *amor fati*) and the affirmation of unconditioned freedom (Fichte's "Be!"), between the Objective and the Subjective, Non-Ego and Ego, Nature and Mind. At the close of a very tense discussion with Hegel, Schelling—like Hölderlin, moreover, at around the same moment—suddenly feels authorized to state that only "true art, or rather the divine (*theion*) in art," "what is most sublime in art" is capable of *objectivizing intellectual intuition*: which is to effectuate the *impossible* as such, according to Kant, the intuition of the Idea (or of the Absolute), the "mad" and excessive transgression of finitude. The first Letter thus gives a glimpse of this absolutely paradoxical possibility. The final one establishes it, in terms to which Schelling will long remain faithful; and in which one immediately recognizes a terminology that came directly from Rousseau (Schelling asks the *same* initial question) and, consequently, from Aristotle:

> It has often been asked how Greek reason could *bear* [my emphasis] the contradictions of Greek tragedy. A mortal, destined by fate to become a criminal and himself fighting *against* such a *fatum*, is nevertheless appallingly punished for the crime, although it was the work of destiny! The *ground* of this contradiction, that which made the contradiction *bearable* [again my emphasis], lay deeper than one would seek it. It lay in the conflict between human freedom and the power of the objective world, in which the mortal must succumb *necessarily* if that power is a superior power[3]—a *fatum*. And yet he must be *punished* for succumbing because he did not succumb *without a fight*. The fact that the criminal, who succumbed only to the superior power of fate, was *punished*, this tragic fact was the recognition of human freedom; it was the *honor* due to freedom. Greek tragedy honored human freedom

by letting its hero *fight* against the superior power fate. *In order not to go beyond the limits of art* [here again my emphasis], the tragedy had to let him *succumb*. Nevertheless, in order to make restitution for this humiliation that *art imposed on human freedom* [my emphasis], it had to let him *atone* even for a crime committed through *fate*.

I interrupt here, for a moment, the reading of this text. It is clear that if tragedy was trying to "reconcile," as Schelling is going to say in a moment, liberty and *fatum* (or "superior power," *Übermacht*), it is because it was an *art*, a (re)presentation: the *Darstellung des Tragischen*, as Hölderlin will write nearly ten years later, which is the (re)presentation of Contradiction itself. And in fact even if "Greek tragedy was unable to reconcile [*zusammenreimen*, make rhyme together; Hölderlin will use the same lexicon] freedom and downfall [*Untergang*]," it does not change the fact that "it was a *great* thought, to suffer punishment willingly even for an inevitable crime, and so to prove one's freedom by the very loss of this freedom, and to go down with a declaration of free will" (193). Schelling adds, moreover, "Here too, as in all instances, Greek art is a *rule*. No people has been more faithful than the Greeks to the essence of humanity, even in art" (193).

No "Rousseauian" weakness, then. No slightly silly (and not simply "naive") recrimination against

Representation, Stage, Theater, Spectacle—and all its commodification.[4] . . . A defense, on the contrary, and the very clearest possible kind, of art (of *tekhnē*). Coupled, moreover, with a terrible warning.

Schelling explains that as long as man *represents* the object, in the Cartesian sense, "he is master of nature . . . just as he [is] master of himself": "he has nothing to fear, for he himself has set limits to it [the object]." But "as soon as he himself has strayed beyond the limit of representation [and it is of course a question of *Vorstellung* here], he finds himself lost. The terrors of the objective world befall him. He has done away with its bounds; how shall he now subdue it?"

This is the anxious question of the *horror* of the world: *die Gräuel*. Of *terror* in general, or of the Terrible: *das Schreckliche* (*to deinon*, as Sophocles says; *das Ungeheure*, as Hölderlin translates—or *das Unheimliche*, as Heidegger retranslates). Or if you prefer, it is the question of danger (*Gefahr*) that Hölderlin, again, continually evoked during the same period; and which Heidegger, again, will define as "the threat that beings pose to being itself."[5] The threat par excellence: of disappearance and destruction, annihilation, death, the manifestation of the non-manifestable itself: *negativity*. The haunting obsession here is, already, that of *evil*.

Schelling asks (these lines were written the very year when Schiller began publishing his essays on the "Naïve" and the "Sentimental"):

What people are more natural than the Greeks, as long as Greek art remains within the limits of nature? Yet, as soon as it leaves those limits, what people are more terrible?

(Schelling here inserts a note that, by the very virulence of the refusal that it demonstrates regarding any alleviating religious or meta-physical "promise," deserves to be read. A sort of *paradoxy* reaches a high point here, which illuminates with a harsh light the truth of the tragic dialectic and which is indispensable to the understanding of its finality: "The Greek gods were still within nature. Their power was not *invisible*, not out of reach of human freedom. Human shrewdness often won a victory over the physical power of the gods. The very bravery of Greek heroes often terrified the Olympians. But for the Greeks the supernatural realm begins with fate, the invisible power out of reach of every natural power, a power upon which even the immortal gods cannot prevail. The more terrible we find the Greeks in the realm of the supernatural, the more natural they are themselves. The more sweetly a people dreams of the supersensuous world, the more despicable, the more unnatural it is itself.")

Then Schelling continues, answering the question at hand. In two parts. On the one hand, he explains, "The invisible power is too sublime to be bribed by adulation; their heroes are too noble to be saved by cowardice. There is nothing left but to fight and fall [*Kampf und Unter-*

gang]"; and this answer applies to that of which tragedy is the *mimēsis*: the *sustasis tōn pragmatōn*, or the drama. On the other hand, however, this answer applies to the tragic effect (*katharsis*, then) and the disastrous consequences that would ensue in its absence or suppression, meaning the absence or suppression of any (re)presentative *limit*, of the very *factum* of *mimēsis*:

> But such a fight is thinkable only for the purpose of tragic art. It could not become a system of action if only because such a system would presuppose a *race of titans* [my emphasis], and because, without this presupposition, it would lead to the complete ruin of humanity.

And in order for the warning, which in 1795 was obviously not (already) addressed to Germany, but more plausibly to the French Revolution, to be even clearer (or, I would gladly say, to make sure one understands that a "people of gods," à la Rousseau, in reality masks, if we do away with theater, a "race of titans"), Schelling insists:

> If it were really the destiny of our race to be tormented by the terrors of an invisible world, would it not be easier to tremble at the faintest notion of freedom, cowed by the superior power of that world, instead of going down fighting? In fact, the *horrors of the present world* [my emphasis] would torment us more than the terrors of a world to come. The man who would obtain his existence in the supersensuous world by

begging for it, will become the *tormentor of humanity in this world, raging against himself and others* [my emphasis]. Power in this world will compensate him for the humiliation in the other one. Waking up from the delights of that world, he returns into this one to make it a hell.

Schelling is doubtless also thinking of the consequences of a certain Christianity. A final sentence closes this development: "It would be fortunate were he to be lulled in the arms of that world to the point of becoming a mere moral *child* in this." And a sentence like this probably owes nothing to prudence.

It is nonetheless the case, and this is the essential part, that the "rule," or even the Law that Schelling establishes—or, more precisely, *recalls* (it comes from Aristotle, and is the speculative translation of *Poetics*, 6)—states, in the clearest and most vigorous possible manner, that *any denial of (re)presentation gives rise to Terror.* And that *katharsis*, more untranslatable than ever, is that of the "drive" toward death, destruction, annihilation, murder, etc. Or toward pain, or "passion," brought on by misfortune and spite, by suffering in general. And we then understand why tragedy offers the first model of the speculative dialectic: *mimēsis* does not only have the pure transcendental power to "make the impossible possible," as Schelling will say of the work of art at the end of his *System of Transcendental Idealism*, in 1800; but *katharsis* itself is—necessarily—transcendental, in the order of human *praxis*: it makes possible the ordeal that cannot be undergone [*l'inéprouvable épreuve*], the impossible experience of an-nihilation and of no-thingness, of death *itself*—"if that is what we want to call this unreality."[6]

A (very) last word, however. It will fall to Hegel, no doubt, to formalize this tragic pattern of speculative thought, which, at bottom, is nothing but the rigorous sublation of the unstable and improbable Rousseauian festival, which precisely did not manage to replace the Stage, the Theater, or, in short, unsublatable *mimēsis*. We remember the reading of the *Eumenides*, in 1801, and its triumphant conclusion. When "the Athena of Athens" saves Orestes, but orders a place to be reserved to the Erinyes of vengeance and murder, at the foot of the Acropolis, Hegel speaks of "reconciliation" and of "sacrifice," necessary to "ethical life" itself, to *Sittlichkeit*. He paraphrases Aristotle:

This reconciliation lies precisely in the knowledge [*Erkenntnis*] of necessity, and in the right which ethical life concedes to its inorganic nature, and to the subterranean powers by making over and sacrificing to them one part of itself. For the force of the sacrifice lies in facing and objectifying the involvement with the inorganic. This involvement is dissolved by being faced; the inorganic is separated and, recognized for what it is, is itself taken up [this is the *logos* itself of the onto-logical] into in-difference [identity] while the living, by placing into the inorganic what it knows to be a part of itself and surrendering it to death [here it is question of the *thesis* of the negative], has all at once recognized the right of the inorganic and *cleansed* [*gereinigt*] itself of it.

This is nothing else but the performance [*Aufführung*, execution, staging], on the ethical plane [*in dem Sittliche*], of the tragedy which the Absolute eternally enacts [*spielt*] with itself, by eternally giving birth to itself into objectivity, submitting in this objective form [*Gestalt*] to suffering [*Leiden*] and death, and rising from its ashes into glory [*Herrlichkeit*].[7]

A little later, in 1806, the same "triumphalism" will be expressed, with the same stylistic power, *but without the reminder of the conditions of theater or of mimēsis*, in the indefinitely quoted passage of the preface to the *Phenomenology of Spirit*. The fact is that already (it never takes very long), the Christian-Lutheran model of "God himself is dead"—which barely reached the surface in the 1801 article ("Passion and Death"), alongside the myth of the Phoenix, and will take its place, just before Absolute Knowledge, in the chapter on "Revealed Religion"—has supplanted the tragic model. We know what comes after. . . . I recall this text, all the same, in the translation that Bataille used, namely the one by Jean Hyppolite (revisited by Kojève):

Death—if we wish so to name that unreality—is the most terrible thing there is and to uphold the work of death is the task which demands the greatest strength. Impotent beauty [in other words: art] hates this awareness, because understanding makes this demand of beauty, a requirement which beauty cannot fulfill. No, the life of Spirit is not that life which is frightened of death and spares itself destruction, but that life which assumes death and lives with it. Spirit attains its truth only by finding itself in absolute dismemberment. It is not that (prodigious) power by being the Positive that turns away from the Negative, as when we say of something: this is nothing or (this is) false and, having (thus) disposed of it, pass from there to something else; no, Spirit is that power only to the degree in which it contemplates the Negative face to face (and) dwells with it. This prolonged sojourn is the magical force which transposes the negative into given-Being.[8]

It was precisely Bataille who wondered whether the "universal practice of sacrifice" explains Hegel at bottom or whether, instead, it is Hegel who provides the rationale for sacrifice (of death (re)presented, "spectacularized," and assuming "identification," as Rousseau says, with the "suffering animal" put to death), and who exclaims: "But this is a comedy!" "This way of seeing can rightly be considered comic." Or else: "In order to express appropriately the situation Hegel got himself into, no doubt involuntarily, one would need the tone, or at least, in a restrained from, the horror of tragedy. But things would quickly take on a comic appearance." Or again, this time regarding the Passion itself, in its Lutheran version: "However that may be, the passage through death is so absent from the divine figure that a myth situated in the tradition associated death, and the agony of death, with the eternal and unique God of the Judeo-Christian sphere. The death of Jesus partakes of comedy to the extent that one cannot without arbitrariness introduce the forgetting of his eternal divinity—which belongs to him—into the consciousness of an omnipotent and infinite God."

Denying (re)presentation—denying theater—is a "comedy."

I do not wish here to enter into a commentary on Bataille, at bottom the most faithful of the Aristotelians of this age. I would just like to give yet again, in order (not) to finish, the following well-known passage, which will provisionally close my remarks. Bataille has just mentioned what he calls the "subterfuge" of sacrificial identification. It is then, in fact, that he exclaims: "But this is a comedy!" And he adds:

At least it would be a comedy if some other method existed which could reveal to the living the invasion of death. . . . This difficulty proclaims the necessity of *spectacle*, or of *representation* in general, without the practice of which it would be possible for us to remain alien and ignorant in respect to death, just as beasts apparently are. Indeed, nothing is less animal than fiction, which is more or less separated [*éloignée*] from the real, from death.

Man does not live by bread alone, but also by the comedies with which he willingly deceives himself. In man it is the animal, it is the natural being, which eats. But man takes part in rites and performances. Or else he can read: to the extent that it is sovereign—authentic—literature prolongs in him the haunting magic of performances, tragic or comic.

In tragedy, at least, it is a question of our identifying with some character who dies, and of believing that we die, although we are alive. Furthermore, pure and simple imagination suffices, but it has the same meaning as the classic subterfuges, performances or books, to which the masses have recourse.[9]

There you have it. There is no better way to say it.

And Rousseau, who was well attuned to these questions, had *almost* said it.

Montpellier, June 2001

NOTES

The translator would like to thank Marlon Jones for his assistance with this translation and Patrick Lyons for help in tracking down the translated versions of a number of Lacoue-Labarthe's quotations.

PART I, CHAPTER 1

[It is worth noting at the outset that the French word *scène* in the title of Part I can mean both "scene" and "stage"; the latter translation will be used more frequently in Part II. —Trans.]

1. Martin Heidegger, *Hölderlins Hymnen "Germanien" und "Der Rhein"*, Gesamtausgabe (GA) vol. 39 (Frankfurt: Vittorio Klostermann, 1980), 51, 74; in English: *Hölderlin's Hymns "Germania" and "The Rhine"*, trans. William McNeill and Julia Ireland (Bloomington: Indiana University Press, 2014), 49–50,

67–68. [This translation will be quoted with minor modifications where required by the language of the French version as given by Lacoue-Labarthe; hereafter both German and English editions will be cited as "HH" followed by the page numbers in the German then in the English. Note that the English translation includes the German pagination at the top of each page. —Trans.]

2. Friedrich Hölderlin, "The Rhine." [Lacoue-Labarthe reproduces the translation of this strophe (slightly modified) from the French version by Gustave Roud: Hölderlin, *Oeuvres* (Paris: Gallimard, Pléiade edition, 1967), 853. His evocation of "readability" requires as clear and straightforward an English version as possible; to that end, I consulted both the version given in HH 250–251, and Michael Hamburger's "plain prose translations" in Hölderlin, *Selected Verse* (Baltimore: Penguin Books, 1961), 166. —Trans.]

3. It must be noted in passing that the elegy "Bread and Wine" is devoted less to the figure of Christ than to that of Dionysos himself, understood as Dio-nysos ("son of Zeus") and, consequently, just like Christ, considered a "hero" or a "demigod." And note as well that Heinse's *Ardinghello*, which does in fact weigh very heavily on Hölderlin's Hyperion, was always taken, even within the circle of the young Marx, as a sort of "communist manifesto," in the sense that this term could have among the radical *rousseauistes* in

France (Babeuf, Restif de la Bretonne) or elsewhere in Europe, particularly in Germany and Italy, during the last decade of the eighteenth century . . . The question, as we will see, is always one of knowing what Heidegger wanted (precisely) to know.

4. For the critique of Rousseau, see in particular the analysis presented by Jeffrey Andrew Barash of the unpublished seminar of 1934–35 in collaboration with Eric Wolf. There Heidegger opposes the "abstract" conception of the state and of "individual liberty" on which *The Social Contract* is based, to the properly historical conception of the political (of the *polis*), in the sense of the History of Spirit, that Hegel elaborates in *The Philosophy of Right*. J. A. Barash, *Heidegger et son siècle: temps de l'être, temps de l'histoire* (Paris: PUF, 1995), 131ff.

5. See in particular the first course on *Nietzsche: Der Wille zur Macht als Kunst* (1936–1937), GA 43. English: Martin Heidegger, *Nietzsche, Volume 1: The Will to Power as Art*, trans. David Farrell Krell (New York: Harper & Row, 1979).

6. I will return to this question, more than once. But I would like to note right away that in numerous texts such as "The Essay on the Origin of Languages" or the *Dictionary of Music*, Rousseau refers constantly to Greek music and to a Greek age that are prior to the Sophists and the Philosophers. Jean Starobinski, in the "Présentation" of the *Essai sur l'origine des langues*, which he edited for the "Bibliothèque de la Pléiade"

edition (see also the edition published in the "Folio Essais" series [Paris: Gallimard, 1990]), insists very rightly on this point. It is indeed this sort of "Hellenophilia" that Hölderlin recognizes in Rousseau (who is thus associated very often in his "mythology" with Dionysos, and is indeed thought as a "mediator" between past and future, Ancients and Moderns, Greece and Hesperia). It is remarkable that on numerous occasions Heidegger cites, with evident jubilation, the famous verses: "and signs [*Winke*] are / Since always the language of the gods," without ever pointing out that these lines are from the sketch of the ode entitled precisely "Rousseau" (see Hölderlin, "Rousseau," in *Poems and Fragments*, trans. Michael Hamburger [London: Anvil Press, 2004], 179).

7. [Full title: *Gedanken über die Nachahmung der Griechischen Werke in der Malerei und Bildhauerkunst* (1755) (Thoughts on the Imitation of Greek Works in Painting and Sculpture). —Trans.]

8. See, among other instances, *Parmenides*, GA 54, 103–104 and 134–135; *Die Grundfragen der Philosophie*, GA 45, 43; and of course *Nietzsche I*. Humboldt is also counted among the "thinkers of History."

9. "Vom Wesen und Begriff der *phusis*," *Wegmarken*, GA 9. English: "On the Essence and Concept of *phusis*," in *Pathmarks*, ed. William McNeill (Cambridge: Cambridge University Press, 1998), 183–230.

10. Jean Beaufret, "Hölderlin et Sophocle," Introduction to Hölderlin, *Remarques sur Oedipe—Remarques*

sur Antigone, French trans. François Fédier (Paris: UGE, 1965).

11. See "On the Essence and Concept of *phusis*," 217 and 222.

12. See "The Origin of the Work of Art," in *Off the Beaten Track*, ed. and trans. Julian Young and Kenneth Haynes (Cambridge: Cambridge University Press, 2002). It is clear in these texts that *tekhnē* (World) "decrypts" *phusis* (Earth).

13. See "The Courage of Poetry" and "The Spirit of National Socialism and Its Destiny."

14. See, for example Kant, "Conjectural Beginning of Human History," and Friedrich Schiller, *Letters on the Aesthetic Education of Man* and "Naive and Sentimental Poetry." The intuition is already present in Rousseau, but it was Schiller who explicitly translated the difference between Nature and Culture into historical terms: Ancients and Moderns. And historico-aesthetic terms: naive and sentimental.

PART I, CHAPTER 2

1. References to the *Discourse on Inequality* in what follows are to Rousseau, *Discourse on the Origin and the Foundations of Inequality Among Men*, in *The First and Second Discourses, Together with Replies to Critics, and Essay on the Origin of Languages*, ed. Victor Gourevitch (New York: Harper & Row, 1990). [Hereafter cited as "DI" followed by the page number.]

The analyses that follow were developed in a course first given at the University of California, Irvine, in 1979 on the mimetology of Diderot and Rousseau (See "Diderot: Paradox and Mimesis," in *Typography: Mimesis, Philosophy, Politics*, ed. Christopher Fynsk (Cambridge: Harvard University Press, 1989) and pursued further in 1985 and 1989 at Berkeley. More recent seminars (Strasbourg, 1995–1996; Mannheim, 1999; Rio de Janeiro, 2000) are at the origin of their current presentation.

2. The implicit reference (to the "inner sense") is in fact contained in the explicit one (to Buffon). Rousseau thus introduces the long quotation that he takes from *Natural History*, IV, "On the Nature of Man": "With the very first step I take, I confidently lean on one of those authorities that are respectable to Philosophers because they are due to a solid and sublime reason which philosophers alone are capable of discovering and appreciating." We must keep in mind at least this much of the quoted text, which at bottom he will continually paraphrase: "However much it may be in our interest to know ourselves, I wonder whether we do not know better everything that is not ourselves. Provided by nature with organs destined exclusively for our preservation, we use them only to receive foreign impressions, we seek only to spread outward, and to exist outside ourselves; too busy multiplying the functions of our senses and extending the external

scope of our being, we rarely use that internal sense which reduces us to our true dimensions, and sets off from us everything that does not belong to it. Yet this is the sense we must use if we wish to know ourselves; it is the only one by which we can judge ourselves . . ." (DI, 200–201, notes 1 and 2).

3. Starobinski here provides a note to the effect that Rousseau evidently misunderstands the rigorous determination of the Aristotelian concept of "nature." Quoting the famous passage from the *Politics* on the *zōon politikon*, he indicates that the nature of a being or of a thing is in its finality and its "end"; and that Rousseau, for his part, "will deny the sociability of man." He nonetheless concedes that, when Rousseau associates "nature" with "the origin," he returns to the original sense of the concept, insofar as Aristotle himself calls for a "genetic" analysis: "Rousseau rigorously followed this method by giving the word 'origin' (*arkhē*) a definition in which logical antecedence necessarily entails *historical* antecedence." However, the entire question, it seems to me, is whether Rousseau's gesture, in its greatest rigor, does not consist precisely in going farther back than any empirical (and therefore historical) genesis in order to interrogate the very origin of history, the perhaps unassignable moment of the negation of nature. See Starobinski, "L'inclinaison du l'axe du globe," in Rousseau, *Essai sur l'origine des langues* (Paris: Gallimard, Folio edition, 1990), 173.

4. Rousseau, *Émile*, IV ("Profession de foi du Vicaire savoyard"), *Oeuvres complètes* (1984), IV:600.

5. Ibid., 952.

6. Which is after all the most consequential determination of the question "Why?" in its so to speak definitive and canonical philosophical formulation, that of Leibniz (at least as Heidegger understands it, between "What Is Metaphysics?" and *The Principle of Reason*). But this is on condition, if I may say, of hearing in the "Why?" the Latin *per quid*, which is not the *ex quo*: neither the "because of which" nor the "in view of which," but rather indeed the "*by* what," "what must be in order that," "what is indispensable (or necessary) so that"; which one can translate "under what condition?" The transcendental question is the true posing of the question "Why?" and Kant represents, from this perspective, the truth of Leibniz.

7. I am referring here to a work in progress on Maurice Blanchot, a part of which has been published under the title "Fidelités" in the collection of essays drawn from the Cérisy conference devoted to Jacques Derrida in 1997, *L'animal autobiographique* (Paris: Galilée, 1998). [For an English translation, see "Fidelities" in *Ending and Unending Agony: On Maurice Blanchot*, trans. Hannes Opelz (New York: Fordham University Press, 2015), 29–45.]

8. See Starobinski, "L'inclinaison de l'axe du globe," 165ff.

1. It is here—and this has been necessary for quite some time—that a serious analysis of what Kant draws from Rousseau when in the third *Critique* he speaks of "the technique of nature." This analysis is implicitly produced Gérard Lebrun's last article, "Oeuvre de l'art et oeuvre d'art," *Philosophie* 63 (Paris: Minuit, 1999). [*Survie* ordinarily means survival. In this context the hyphenation implies a kind of "over-life," not in the sense of greater life or something beyond and other than life, but a depropriating excess of life, a life added to or supplementing life, a "meta-" life in technics. —Trans.]

2. "We seek to know only because we desire to enjoy" (DI 149).

3. See Rousseau, *Letter to d'Alembert on the Theater*, in *Collected Writings of Rousseau*, vol. 10, *Letter to d'Alembert and Writings for the Theater*, eds. Allan Bloom, Charles Butterworth, Christopher Kelly (Hanover: University Press of New England, 2004), 309–310; Diderot, *Paradoxe sur le comédien* (Paris: Garnier-Flammarion, 1967), 127–128, 131, 156, 163. I will return to this point.

4. [*Jouer*: play, also in the sense of acting. —Trans.]

5. It is obviously not the same scene being repeated, but everything happens as if a "primal scene" was always and everywhere necessary: the scene of the fountains in chapter IX of the *Essay on the Origin of Languages*; the scene of the harvest in *Julie, or the New*

Heloise; the scene of the "Regiment of Saint-Gervais" in the *Letter to M. d'Alembert*; the scene of the accident in the "Second Walk" of the *Reveries*, etc. (there are others). It would be necessary to enumerate and analyze them systematically.

6. See Starobinski's note in the French "Folio" edition of the Second Discourse, 186–187. We must also refer back to the two notes from the Introduction and the text itself of the *Essay* (*Oeuvres complètes*, V:cci–cciii and 1559–1561), as well as, of course, the analyses developed by Starobinski in the *Le remède dans le mal* (Paris: Gallimard, 1989).

7. And yet, despite this shrinking back, Rousseau will always hold to a certain originarity of *transport*, as attested no less by the *Essay* than by *Emile*. Derrida and Starobinski have stated the essential on this subject; I will not go back over this. Except to say that Hölderlin, in his theory of "tragic transport," will perhaps remember this. But I have discussed this question elsewhere. [See especially Lacoue-Labarthe, "The Caesura of the Speculative," in *Typography: Mimesis, Philosophy, Politics* (Stanford: Stanford University Press, 1989), 208–235, and "The Theater of Hölderlin," in *Philosophy and Tragedy*, eds. Miguel de Beistegui and Simon Sparks (New York: Routledge, 2000), 115–135).]

8. This is particularly clear in the first paragraph of chapter IX of the *Essay on the Origin of Languages*.

9. We must be very clear about this hypothesis: it does not amount to saying that Aristotelian poetics of

tragedy can be comprehended only *politically*. (And yet . . .) But it does amount to saying that the philosophico-political debate inaugurated already in the Renaissance—at the time of the *real* collapse of the theologico-political—by Machiavelli, *for example*, is inseparable from an *anxious* reading of the *Poetics*. A reading that, *retrospectively*, perhaps enlightens us about the *Poetics* in question. I do not mean, therefore, that Rousseau is commenting Aristotle here (and yet . . .), but that Rousseau—along with a few others, obviously—illuminates Aristotle. They give us to *think* what is at stake in the *Poetics*. Put another way, and more brutally, a retrospective reading of Aristotle is probably necessary. This reading would have some chance of illuminating, in turn, modern political philosophy. Including Marx and Freud, if we consent to read them.

I must add here that Rousseau, without any coincidence, indeed sets in opposition, in *Emile* (*Oeuvres complètes*, IV:506), "positive or attractive action" and "negative or repulsive action." Or love and hate, if you prefer: attraction and repulsion. The idea is already present in the *Essay*, chapter II, regarding the "passionate" origin of language: "The passions all bring men together, but the necessity of seeking their livelihood makes them flee one another. Neither hunger nor thirst, but love, hatred, pity, anger wrested the first voices from them." *Essay on the Origin of Languages*, in *The Collected Writings of Rousseau*, vol. 7, *Essay on the*

Origin of Languages and Writings Related to Music, ed. John T. Scott (Hanover: University Press of New England, 1998), 294. This is exactly what is at issue here.

10. See "Hölderlin and the Greeks," in *Typography: Mimesis, Philosophy, Politics*.

11. He barely even "cites" them, here or there, in his courses; and always, as we could show without any difficulty, in a "tendentious" (not to say scandalous) fashion. I cannot linger on this point here.

12. I am thinking of the book that one could call "impressive," despite its strange rancor, by Domenico Losurdo, *Heidegger and the Ideology of War: Community, Death, and the West*, trans. Jon and Marella Morris (New York: Humanity Books, 2001).

13. [*Dérapage*: a slip or a faux pas, but also a skidding out of control. —Trans.]

PART II, CHAPTER 1

1. [For the occurrence of this passage in the *Letter to d'Alembert*, see Rousseau, *Collected Writings of Rousseau*, vol. 10, *Letter to d'Alembert and Writings for the Theater*, ed. Allan Bloom, Charles Butterworth, and Christopher Kelly (Hanover: University Press of New England, 2004), 268. The *Letter to d'Alembert* will henceforth be cited as "LA" followed by the page number of this volume. —Trans.]

2. Nor does it owe anything to the Pastors of Geneva. The sole reference—included *in extremis* as a

note (LA 262–263)—to the *Instruction Chrétienne*, is just to indicate that if there are "blameworthy" spectacles, we can conceive of others "where agreeable and useful lessons for every station in life can even be presented." This is hardly compromising . . . Henceforth, at the very least, the essential is granted, namely that "the Theater is made for the *people*" (my emphasis).

3. Rousseau does not deny for a moment the aforementioned "Socinianism," meaning the refusal— which, by the way, does not distance him much from d'Alembert—to adhere or subscribe to dogmas judged perfectly irrational, namely what are essentially Catholic dogmas (Trinity, divinity of Jesus, etc.). In the passage from there to calling the reformed church a "sect" and speaking in terms of "heresy," there is nonetheless a line that he considers it scandalous to cross.

4. See *On Theatrical Imitation*, in *The Collected Writings of Rousseau*, vol. 7, *Essay on the Origin of Languages and Writings Related to Music*, ed. and trans. John T. Scott (Hanover: University Press of New England, 2000), 337–350 (hereafter cited as "TI" followed by the page number of this volume).

5. The brief introductory "Notice" deserves to be quoted here in its entirety:

This short Writing is merely a kind of extract of various places where Plato treats theatrical

Imitation. I hardly had any other part in it other than that of having assembled and connected them into the form of a continuous discourse instead of that of the Dialogue which they had in the original. The occasion for this labor was the Letter to M. d'Alembert on the Theatre; but not having been able to fit it into that work comfortably, I put it aside in order to use it elsewhere or to suppress it entirely. Since then, having left my hands, this writing happened to be involved—I know not how—in a transaction which did not concern me. The Manuscript has been returned to me, but the Bookseller has demanded it back as acquired by him in good faith, and I do not want to gainsay the person who gave it to him. This is how this bagatelle makes its way today into Print. (TI 337)

One will notice, among other things, Rousseau's loose treatment of the Platonic *lexis* itself. The use of the mimetic mode to condemn the mimetic mode does not seem to be of any concern to him, at least not here.

6. The concord here is evidently between reason and sensibility.

7. [The French word *spectacle* is often translated in Rousseau as "theater" (as in the first instance in the long quotation in note 5) or "entertainment" (the latter being the choice in the translation of the *Letter to d'Alembert* used here). This should be kept in mind as

I have not systematically altered the translations on this point, but have, however, translated Lacoue-Labarthe's use of the word literally, given its specific resonance with certain aspects of his argument. On the use of the word "stage" later in this sentence and elsewhere, see the previous note in Part I on the translation of *scène* as "scene" or "stage." —Trans.]

8. The argument of the Stoic is a traditional one, but Rousseau borrows it directly from Du Bos.

9. See LA 262. Rousseau writes: "At the first glance given to these institutions I see immediately that the Theater is a form of amusement; and if it is true that amusements are necessary to man, you will at least admit that they are only permissible insofar as they are necessary, and that every useless amusement is an evil for a Being whose life is so short and whose time is so precious. The state of man has its pleasures which are derived from his nature and are born of his labors, his relations, and his needs. And these pleasures, sweeter to the one who tastes them in the measure that his soul is healthier, make whoever is capable of participating in them indifferent to all others. A Father, a son, a Husband, and a Citizen have such cherished duties to fulfill that they are left nothing to give to boredom. The good use of time makes time even more precious, and the better one puts it to use, the less one can find to lose. Thus it is constantly seen that the habit of work renders inactivity intolerable and that a good conscience extinguishes the taste for frivolous pleasures.

But it is discontent with one's self, the burden of idleness, the neglect of simple and natural tastes, that makes foreign amusement so necessary. I do not like the need to occupy the heart constantly with the Stage as if it were ill at ease inside of us." We see without difficulty that these few lines implicitly program the "civic festival" that Rousseau recommends *in fine* (I will come back to this point).

10. See LA 306, and especially 309–310: These are the pages that Diderot will "take on" in the *Paradox of the Comedian*. Through the counterexample of the orator, it appears clearly here that Rousseau has retained the lesson from Plato on the *haplē diēgēsis*, or the analogous but "neutral" formal distinctions of Aristotle (*Poetics*, 3). Rousseau writes: "The Orator and the Preacher, it could be said, make use of their persons as well does the Actor. The difference is, however, very great. When the Orator appears in public, it is to speak and not to Show himself off; he represents only himself; he fills only his own role, speaks only in his own name, says, or ought to say, only what he thinks; the man and the role being the same, he is in his place; he is in the situation of any citizen who fulfils the function of his estate" (LA 310).

11. See LA 343ff. The implicit reference here to Jean-Luc Nancy is in no way coincidental. There is, moreover, in Rousseau's work, if not what I have elsewhere labeled a "national aestheticism" (the political idea of a nation only barely emerges), at least a

sort of "cantonal aestheticism" or, to be more serious, the announcement of what Hegel will conceive as the "subjective-objective moment" of Greek art: the Polity itself. Rousseau's role was not inconsiderable in the long history of the poietic conception of politics, as was highlighted by Hannah Arendt and then, following her lead, by Jacques Taminiaux.

12. [In English in the original. —Trans.]

13. Aristotle, *Poetics*, trans. Anthony Kenny (Oxford: Oxford University Press, 2013).

14. One can consult on this point the very useful history of the reception of the *Poetics* that Michel Magnien recapitulates in the second part of the Introduction to his annotated translation of the text: Aristotle, *Poétique* (Paris: LGF, 1990).

15. As Jean Rousset notes in his edition of the text, Rousseau was not the first to express doubt about this "rule": "Corneille and Fontenelle had said as much"; and he also mentions Voltaire, in his *Commentaire sur Corneille*, from which Rousseau seems nearly to repeat this formulation: "For the purgation of the passions, I know nothing of this medicine." Rousseau, *Oeuvres complètes*, vol. 5, *Ecrits sur la musique, la langue et le théâtre* (Paris: Gallimard, Pléiade edition, 1995), 1317.

16. The nuance is almost imperceptible. The question must nonetheless be asked—which, unfortunately, the two editors of the *Poetics* to which I refer do not do, although at the same time, in terms of the analysis of *katharsis*, I find myself in agreement with them. To

take a simple example: in the *kommos* of *Antigone*, does Antigone pity herself? Or why, at the end of *Oedipus Rex*, does Oedipus, pitiable a moment earlier, fly into such a (frightening) rage against Creon? In both cases, we are dealing with "monsters," as Rousseau puts it, and besides Oedipus he mentions Phaedra and Medea. And we see that, at bottom, it is the whole famous question of *identification* that is posed here: does *katharsis* suppose it?

17. On this point as well I subscribe to the previously quoted commentary by Dupont-Roc and Lallot (see, in particular, 191–193).

18. See *The Birth of Tragedy*, chapter XXII. It goes without saying that likewise nothing justifies the "religious" (cultic or ritual) interpretation of *katharsis* either. Even when, in book VIII of the *Politics*, Aristotle speaks of "possessive" melodies (*enthousiastikai*), apt to provoke a trance, he does not seem to be referring to this. He treats them in any case on the same level as the other "ethical" or "practical" ones.

19. All the texts quoted in what follows are taken from LA 263–270.

20. ["Entertainment" here translates *spectacle*. See note 7 in this chapter on the use of these terms in Lacoue-Labarthe's text and in the *Letter*. —Trans.]

21. [A reference to Corneille, *Illusion comique* (1636). —Trans.]

1. This is the first—and last—time that Rousseau quotes Aristotle "directly" (in reality, he takes this Latin quotation from the *Poetics*, 1448, and its paraphrase, from Muralt, which he also uses, in *Julie, or the New Heloise*, for certain letters by Saint-Preux written from Paris; see note by Jean Rousset, in *Oeuvres complètes*, V:1322–1323).

2. [*Comme*: this word includes both of these senses (it is also used in the first sentence of this paragraph, in speaking of imitation *as such*, "*comme telle*"). —Trans.]

3. [The verb Lacoue-Labarthe uses here, as elsewhere, is *relever*, which in the present context is meant as a translation of the Hegelian term *aufheben* (substantive *Aufhebung*). I have therefore rendered it with the conventional neologism *sublate* and variations. —Trans.]

4. I refer here to the celebrated analyses of Peter Szondi, "Le naïf est le sentimental," in *Poésie et poétique de l'idéalisme allemande* (Paris: Minuit, 1975), as well as to certain texts, particularly on Hölderlin, that I collected in *Typography: Mimesis, Philosophy, Politics*. As for the Schillerian theory of theater, I am thinking essentially of the studies of 1791–1793, written simultaneously under the effects of Goethe's *Iphigenia* and Kant's third *Critique*: "Of the Cause of the Pleasure We Derive from Tragic Objects," which takes up again

the conclusions of the course on tragedy given in Jena in 1790, "On tragic art," "On the pathetic." The preface to *The Bride of Messina*, "On the Use of the Chorus in Tragedy" (a text that was written later, in 1803, and that presupposes a reading of the first philological works of Friedrich von Schlegel), poses entirely different problems, as Nietzsche will be the first to recognize in *The Birth of Tragedy*. Schiller draws out Rousseau's consequences so well, in fact, that he launches into a pure and simple rehabilitation of the theater.

5. In Rousseau, *Oeuvres complètes*, III:288.

6. Ibid., V:cxciv (this is Starobinski's Introduction to the *Essai sur l'origine des langues*). Starobinski, as I have indicated already, has suggested elsewhere that this indeed represents the first sketch of the Hegelian *Aufhebung*.

7. When he turns his attention to modern comic theater, Rousseau says explicitly, "Let us take it in its perfection, that is to say, at its birth" (LA 275). And it is Molière that he will discuss.

8. *Poetics*, 11, 1452b–1453a. These are the famous pages where Aristotle examines, in fact, the type of "structure" (*sunthesis*), not the type of "character" or figure, apt to arouse fear and pity: the good must not pass from happiness to unhappiness, nor, inversely, must the wicked [*scélérats*] pass from unhappiness to happiness, for pity can extend only to the man who has not earned his unhappiness, and fear is inspired only

by the unhappiness of one's fellow (*phobos . . . peri ton homoion*). "We are left, then, with the person in between: a man not outstanding in virtue or justice, who falls into adversity not through vice or depravity but because he errs (*hamartia*) in some way. He is a personage enjoying renown and prosperity, such as Oedipus, Thyestes, and eminent persons from families of that kind" (Aristotle, *Poetics*, 13, 1453a). Rousseau avoids direct commentary on the case of Oedipus, but he paraphrases this passage diligently.

9. In the Pléiade edition, Jean Rousset notes that the word *intéressant* (interesting) in the classical sense, means "inspiring compassion" (*Oeuvres complètes*, V:1325).

10. [Lacoue-Labarthe's interpolation; this phrase occurs a few lines later in the same paragraph of Rousseau's *Letter*. —Trans.]

11. Allow me to refer here to my essay, "The Scene Is Primal," trans. Karen McPherson, in *The Subject of Philosophy*, ed. Thomas Trezise (Minneapolis: University of Minnesota Press, 1993), 99–115.

12. We need only refer, to remain with Rousseau's examples, to the mention of Oedipus in the chapter "Being and Appearance" in the *Introduction to Metaphysics*, published in 1935.

13. Rousseau, *Julie, or the New Heloise*, trans. Philip Steward and Jean Vaché (Hanover: Dartmouth College Press, 1997), 206; cited in Jean Rousset's note to this

passage in the Pléiade edition (*Oeuvres complètes*, V:1327).

14. See Jean Rousset's note in the Pléaide edition (*Oeuvres complètes*, V:1350): "Rousseau received on this subject a letter from J.D. LeRoy, author of *Ruines des plus beaux monuments de la Grèce* (1758), in which the theater of Sparta was featured. 'A large part of it still exists, and Pausanias and Plutarch speak of it.' Rousseau responded on November 4, 1758: 'I thank you, sir, for your kindness in alerting me to my error on the subject of the theater of Sparta . . . , I request your permission to use your letter in another edition of my own.' This was duly carried out by the editors of the 1781 edition." But certainly not by most of Rousseau's modern editors.

15. The precaution is not useless for the simple reason that the Spartan dances suppose nudity and, especially, the mixing of genders among young people, and in festivals the use of wine is far from forbidden, etc. As "rigorist" as Rousseau is regarding ("modern") actors and especially actresses, he also argues for relationships without "dissimulation," without *hypocrisy* ("for everything which is bad in morality is also bad in politics" (LA 331)) between the sexes, according to the inclinations and sentiments, the emotions of body or soul: of the heart. And in view, naturally, of marriage. Hence the defense of (popular) dances, which ended up provoking such a scandal. Even the military festival (that of the famous regiment of

Saint-Gervais [LA 351]) does not exclude women; on the contrary.

16. Allow me to refer to my own essays on Hölderlin, *Métaphrasis*, suivi de *Le théâtre de Hölderlin* (Paris: PUF, 1998). [The latter essay has been translated into English as "Hölderlin's Theater," trans. Simon Sparks, in *Philosophy and Tragedy*, eds. Miguel de Beistegui and Simon Sparks (New York: Routledge, 2000), 115–134.]

17. In the first of the two versions of the lecture on "The Origin of the Work of Art" (in the French translation by E. Martineau), we can read the "crudest" (or most brutal) transcription of this formula. Heidegger has just revealed the famous example of the Greek temple, meant to "illustrate" the relationship between "Earth" (*phusis*) and "World" (*tekhnē*): "Everything, here, is *reversed* [my emphasis: *Alles ist da umgekehrt*]: it is the temple, in its standing, which gives things, for the first time, the face thanks to which they will become visible in the future," etc. In short, *tekhnē* unveils *phusis*. "And it is the same," he adds, "for the statue of the god," which "is anything but an image, charged simply to make known the aspect of the god—which no one knows—but a work which 'is' the god itself," etc. He then continues (I modify the translation very slightly): "The same goes again for the work of language—tragedy—; here, nothing is executed [staged: *vorgeführt*], but it is a combat [*der Kampf*, this is in 1935] of the new gods against the old ones that

begins," etc. [interpolations are Lacoue-Labarthe's]. Hegel's "Natural Law" article, his chapter on *Sittlichkeit* in the *Phenomenology of Spirit*, *Philosophy of Right* . . . *The Eumenides*, *Antigone*: we are familiar with all this: the struggle of the new law against the old, of night against day, of the *agora* against the *oikos*, of man (*anēr*) against woman (see Rousseau's fifth argument), of democracy against tyranny, of freedom against servitude: Hegel, to be sure; but Rousseau first of all. The denial of this debt is at least politically clear.

18. The rehabilitation of Greece is a "digression," as Rousseau says. Hardly having finished it ("Let us return to the Romans who, far from following the example of the Greeks in this respect, set an entirely contrary one" [LA 309]), Rousseau returns to his Platonist charge against actors: this is the very famous passage which Diderot will attempt to answer, word for word (allow me to refer once again to my essay on "Diderot: Paradox and Mimesis" in *Typography: Mimesis, Philosophy, Politics*): "What is the talent of the actor? It is the art of counterfeiting himself, of putting on another character than his own, of appearing different than he is, of becoming passionate in cold blood, of saying what he does not think as naturally as if he really did think it, and, finally, of forgetting his own place by dint of taking another's"—etc. (LA 309). There is more: he has not

yet denounced the venality and corruption of actors, the market economy of the theater, the usurpation of social roles (disguising oneself as "King"), the deceit and illusionism; but as we know, the crucial grievance is that "mixture of abjectness, duplicity, ridiculous conceit, and disgraceful abasement which render [the actor] fit for all sorts of roles except for the most noble of all, that of man, which he abandons" (LA 309). The problem is that, unlike the orator, "an Actor on stage, displaying other sentiments than his own, saying only what he is made to say, often representing a chimerical being, annihilates himself, as it were, and is lost in his Hero. And, in this forgetting of the man, if something remains of him, it is used as the plaything of the spectators" (LA 310). Being thus the *negation* of man, the actor—which is to say, "theatrical" *mimēsis*; the last Rousseauians today would say "(commodity) spectacle"; Rousseau would have subscribed to this, including the commodity aspect—is the index of *negativity* in man. It is precisely *this* negativity that the example of the nontheatrical theater of the Greeks would ideally make it possible to "sublate."

19. Regarding Christianity, Rousseau obviously remains very prudent. But in all these pages, as at the beginning of the *Letter*, his reticence, even hostility, is evident. Regarding Rome, in any case, and the Church Fathers: Protestantism *oblige*.

20. The passage, or the equivalence, of "not yet" to "no longer, in the future," already offers the schema, albeit "naively," of the law of *historiality*, as Heidegger formalized it by *repeating* (which is to say, by radicalizing) the Nietzschean conception of "monumental history" (see my "History and Mimesis" in *Typography: Mimesis, Philosophy, Politics*). In all rigor, the law of historiality requires that the uneventuated in the event (in the past) offers the possibility—or the promise—of the to-come (of the future). If Rousseau—and I will touch on this in a moment—was able to believe in the Civic (cantonal) Festival, it is all the same less certain that Heidegger believed in Nuremberg or in the 1936 Games, which is to say the *mises en scène* of Leni Riefenstahl . . . (It is from this angle that one would have to analyze the Revolutionary festivals—of Reason, the Supreme Being, etc.—entrusted to David; but this is not the place).

21. It is doubtless true, as Dupont-Roc and Lallot emphasize in their commentary in the French edition, that nothing authorizes us to see *already* in Aristotle's analysis of *mimēsis* in the *Poetics* a theory of the sublime. This does not change the fact that, starting with Longinus, this theory of the sublime is constituted, almost explicitly, as a paraphrase of Aristotle. I have said a few words on this elsewhere (see "Sublime Truth," in the collective volume *Of the Sublime: Presence in Question*, trans. Jeffrey S. Librett (Albany: SUNY Press: 1993), 71–108.)

22. This, as we recall, is the concluding formula of the note at the very end—or almost—of the *Letter*, where Rousseau evokes the episode of the "Regiment of Saint-Gervais," which I have already mentioned (we could even entitle it, "A childhood memory of Jean-Jacques Rousseau"): the men's dance after the exercise, the military music, the participation of women (first as "Spectators," and then, not limiting themselves to that, going down into the street), and "the children," the "general emotion," the testamentary sentence of the father, seized by a "trembling" that Rousseau believes he can still "feel" and "share": "Jean-Jacques . . . love your country"—all of this leads to a *lesson*: "I am well aware that this *Entertainment* [Spectacle], which moved me so, would be without appeal for countless others; one must have eyes made for seeing it and a heart made for feeling it. *No*, the only *pure* joy is *public* joy, and the true sentiments of *nature* reign only over the *people*. Ah! Dignity, daughter of pride and mother of boredom, have your melancholy Slaves ever had a similar moment in their lives?" (LA 351; my emphases). This could not be clearer.

23. I refer here to the now classic readings by Jean Starobinski, *Jean-Jacques Rousseau: Transparency and Obstruction* (Chicago: University of Chicago Press, 1988), and by Jacques Derrida, *Of Grammatology*, (Baltimore: Johns Hopkins University Press, 1998).

24. Jean Rousset is no doubt correct to say that the long note that Rousseau attaches to the word "useful"

is aimed first of all at the bourgeoisie of Geneva: "influential families, council members, magistrates," who would have feared the cost and harmful effects of plays and festivals among the popular "classes" (*Oeuvres complètes*, V:1376). In its very principle, which is rigorously Platonist, its significance is nonetheless much more general. It is stated here clearly that: 1) pleasure, as much as bread, is necessary to the *life* of the "People" as to the "disposition of the State"; healthy emulation and diversion do not in the least prevent "each man's being satisfied [*se plaise*] in his estate," on the contrary; rivalry springs from "discontentment," "everything goes badly when one aspires to the position of another"; and that 2) "amusements" do not detract at all from work but can very well be conjoined with it, to everyone's greater profit (the example of the Montagnons had already proven it): "If the people have only the time to earn their bread; they must still have some in which to eat it with joy; otherwise they will not earn it for long [. . .]; offer them amusements which make them like their stations and prevent them from craving for a sweeter one." There is little doubt that this rule has not often been violated.

25. Sarah Kofman took on this question in *Le respect des femmes* (Paris: Gallilée, 1996).

26. Once again, we are not only dealing here with an exclusively "poietic" and not "praxic" conception of the state or of politics, which would give birth to Robespierre and Othon de Bavière, Marx and Nietzsche,

Lukacs and Heidegger. In short, "real socialism" and fascism: a "modern" Platonism. This does exist, indeed, but not in Rousseau (Hannah Arendt—and a few others—notwithstanding). Despite the military music of the regiment of Saint-Gervais—and Sparta—despite the socioeconomic worry and the preoccupation with inequality, there is never for a second a question of the *militarization* of society.

27. I refer again to a work on Maurice Blanchot not yet published, but a draft of which was published under the title "Fidélités," in *L'animal autobiographique.* [This work has since been published and translated: see Lacoue-Labarthe, *Ending and Unending Agony: On Maurice Blanchot*, trans. Hannes Opelz (New York: Fordham University Press, 2015). Rousseau is referred to especially in "Fidelities" and "The Contestation of Death." —Trans.]

28. "The Supreme" ("Das Höchste"), from "Pindar Fragments and Commentary," in Hölderlin, *Poems and Fragments*, trans. Michael Hamburger (London: Anvil Press, 2004), 712–713 (translation slightly modified).

29. [I have tried in these formulations to render the sense of *même* as both "itself" and as "same," by which Lacoue-Labarthe means to indicate not the sheer self-identity of a substance, but rather a thing's being-itself insofar as it resembles . . . itself, where this "itself," however, is always also determined in a kind of resemblance or sameness to *other* things that are the

"same" as it, and thus to itself as other. This originarily mimetic sense of "self" and "same" is always inhabited and constituted by the self-othering gap of (re) presentation. —Trans.]

30. [English in original. —Trans.]

31. I am referring of course to Jean-Luc Nancy, *The Speculative Remark (One of Hegel's Bons Mots)*, trans. Céline Surprenant (Stanford: Stanford University Press, 2002).

32. This is Lacan's "translation," in *The Seminar, Book VII. The Ethics of Psychoanalysis, 1959–1960*, ed. Jacques-Alain Miller, trans. Dennis Porter (New York: Norton, 1992), 245. Lacan's hostility toward Hegel (and Bataille, Kojève, et al.)—which, by the way, does not in the least prevent yet another "sanctification" of the "figure" of Antigone, meaning yet another misinterpretation of Sophocles' tragedy—and toward Bernays (Nietzsche, Bataille, et al.) and the onto-physiological theory of "discharge" (*katharsis* as *Entladung*), in short, the will to "supersede," all this means that Lacan does not perceive that "calming" or "lightening [*allègement*]" can translate at the very most the *kouphisis meth' hēdonēs* of the *Politics* (VIII, 1342a), and not even the *kharan ablabē*, the "in-nocent joy" that music provides—about which Rousseau, however, speaks in a very informed and clear fashion. (I take the liberty of referring to a lecture to which I gave the title "De l'esthéthique," but that was published as

"De l'éthique: à propos de l'Antigone" in *Lacan avec les philosophes* [Paris: Albin Michel, 1991]).

PART II, CHAPTER 3

1. Peter Szondi, *An Essay on the Tragic*, trans. Paul Fleming (Stanford: Stanford University Press, 2002), 1. See also Szondi's essay on Hölderlin, "Poétique des genres et philosophie de l'histoire," in *Poésie et poétique de l'idéalisme allemand*, trans. Jean Bollack (Paris: Minuit, 1975), 248–289, a reading of which is constantly presupposed here.

2. I will use here the translation—and remarks—of Jean-François Courtine in his edition of the *Premiers écrits (1794–1795)* (Paris: PUF, 1987), 208–210. [For English, see F. W. J. Schelling, "Philosophical Letters on Dogmatism and Criticism," in *The Unconditional in Human Knowledge: Four Early Essays (1794–1796)*, trans. Fritz Marti (Lewisburg, PA: Bucknell University Press, 1980). All quotes in what follows are from pages 192–194 of this translation. On occasion the translation has been slightly modified in accordance with Lacoue-Labarthe's French quotations. —Trans.] I myself sketched out a commentary on these pages in "Oedipe comme figure," in *L'imitation des modernes: Typographies II* (Paris: Galilée, 1986), 203–225 [English: "Oedipus as Figure," *Radical Philosophy* 118 (March/April 2003): 7–17. —Trans.]

3. "Conflict": *polemos*, *Kampf* or *Streit*; "power,"
"superior power": *Macht*, *Übermacht*: not only is this
already the vocabulary of Nietzsche, it is also that of
Heidegger in 1933–1935.

4. This remark is not directed at Guy Debord, in his
critical rigor that is, but at his "facility," yes—and at
the truly ridiculous exploitation to which, still today, it
has given rise.

5. The formula is found in the 1936 lecture, "Hölder-
lin and the Essence of Poetry," in *Elucidations of
Hölderlin's Poetry*, trans. Keith Hoeller (Amherst, NY:
Humanity Books, 2000), 55; this lecture itself con-
denses the material in the 1934–1935 course *Hölderlin's
Hymns "Germania" and "The Rhine."*

6. [As Lacoue-Labarthe will make clear, this
quotation is from Hegel's "Preface" to *Phenomenology
of Spirit*. —Trans.]

7. Hegel, *Natural Law: The Scientific Ways of Treat-
ing Natural Law, Its Place in Moral Philosophy, and Its
Relation to the Positive Sciences of Law*, trans. T. M.
Knox (Philadelphia: University of Pennsylvania Press,
1975), 104. [All interpolations are Lacoue-Labarthe's.]
If we think of Rousseau's second *Discourse*, this title
("The Scientific Ways of Treating Natural Law . . .") is
in no way indifferent.

8. Quoted in Bataille, "Hegel, Death and Sacrifice,"
trans. Jonathan Strauss, in *The Bataille Reader*, ed. Fred
Botting and Scott Wilson (Oxford: Blackwell Publish-
ers, 1997), 282–283. [This translation of the passage

remains closer to the French translation of Hegel as quoted by Bataille (and referred to by Lacoue-Labarthe), and so has been used here. See also Hegel, *Phenomenology of Spirit*, trans. A. V. Miller (Oxford: Clarendon Press, 1977), 19. —Trans.]

   9. Ibid., 287.